WITHDRAWN
UTSA LIBRARIES

THE HARVEST OF A QUIET EYE

THE HARVEST OF A QUIET EYE

QUIET EYE

A Book of Digressions

BY

ODELL SHEPARD

WITH ILLUSTRATIONS BY
BEATRICE STEVENS

Essay Index Reprint Series

BOOKS FOR LIBRARIES PRESS
FREEPORT, NEW YORK

INTERNATIONAL STANDARD BOOK NUMBER:
0-8369-2428-2

LIBRARY OF CONGRESS CATALOG CARD NUMBER:
77-117843

PRINTED IN THE UNITED STATES OF AMERICA

TO THE INHABITANTS OF

FRIENDSHIP VALLEY

AND ESPECIALLY TO

THE PESSIMIST WITH THE SCYTHE

THE LADIES OF BRISK-TO-HIGH

THE LORD OF VENILY

THE VOICES

THE WITENAGEMOT

THE FARM HORSE ON FURLOUGH

THE PATRIARCH OF NORTH ASHFORD

THE PHILOSOPHERS OF THE BARN FLOOR

THE HOBO

MY LADY OF SUCCOR

THE LONELY MAN

THE SNAKE FIGHTER

THE GOOD CITIZEN

SMITTIE

THE MAJOR

THE READER

TWENTY BROOKS

ONE HUNDRED LANES

AND ALL THE DOGS THAT DID NOT BARK

THESE RANDOM PAGES ARE AFFECTIONATELY DEDICATED

WITH THE HOPE THAT WE MAY MEET AGAIN

O. S.

The outward shows of sky and earth,
Of hill and valley, he has viewed;
And impulses of deeper birth
Have come to him in solitude.

In common things that round us lie
Some random truths he can impart, —
The harvest of a quiet eye
That broods and sleeps on his own heart.

WORDSWORTH

This is what you shall do: love the earth, and sun, and animals, despise riches, stand up for the stupid and crazy, hate tyrants, argue not concerning God, have patience and indulgence towards the people, take off your hat to nothing known or unknown or to any man or number of men, go freely with powerful uneducated persons, re-examine all you have been told at school or church or in any book, and dismiss whatever insults your own soul.

WALT WHITMAN

I WISH to thank the Editors of *The Christian Science Monitor*, *The Boston Evening Transcript*, *The Youth's Companion*, *Contemporary Verse*, *The Bookman*, *The Unpartizan Review*, *The Smart Set*, and *Scribner's Magazine* for permission to reprint parts of this book which first appeared in their pages.

O. S.

CONTENTS

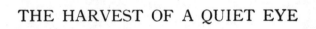

THE HARVEST OF A QUIET EYE

THE
HARVEST OF A QUIET EYE

I

CONNECTICUT THE LITTLE: A PANEGYRIC

*Blessed of the Lorde is this land, for the sweetness of heven,
and of the scee underliende; for the sprynges; for the precious
thinges of the sonne; for the sweetness of the toppes of the oolde
mounteynes, and for the daynties of the hillis that last forever.*
— Anon.

 WHILE turning the pages of a pocket atlas, trying to verify an obscure reference, I came by chance upon a tiny map, four inches wide by two and a half in depth. A shapely little map it was, delicately symmetrical, with its three main southward-flowing rivers, the greatest in the middle, and wide spaces of intervening hills. I saw that the country to the north had bitten tentatively into one boundary line and that the country to the southwest had nibbled at another, but, knowing the masterful ways of those two neighbors and knowing also what their temptation must have been, I could not blame them. These minor indentations were just enough to save the country's contour from a too mathematical regularity without disturbing its admirable proportions. And

the map was colored, appropriately, a sunny green. I felt a thrill of patriotic pride to find that Connecticut looks well even on paper.

All that any one cares to read about the charm of maps and how they marry mathematics to poetry may be read in the books of other men. It is to be observed, furthermore, that the pleasures of map-reading are made out of hope and recollection, so that they are fittest for the February fireside, whereas this book of mine is about real happenings in the autumn. Considering, finally, that the book I am to write will certainly be full, do what I may, of détours and circumambulations, meanders, purple patches, and loose sallies of the mind, I think it best not to divagate in the very first pages, but simply to say that I liked this little map because it was little, because it pictured for me a little land, and because that land was my own.

Neither is this the place in which to inquire profoundly why our affection for some things — such as kittens, for example, and children, rivers, towns, and countries — should vary inversely as their size. Let us say, by way of rough approximation, that they bring into play the 'protective instinct,' suggesting the notion, subtly flattering to our self-love, that they need our assistance, or at least our praise. Small countries, for whatever reasons, have always been most dearly beloved, and this law which made the strength of Attica and of many an Italian city-state is not likely to change in our time of wide-spread territories. What is the outlook, then, for a land so huge that not even the traveling salesman can know it well in every part, unless every man strikes down deep roots of affection in some small and comprehensible district to which he really belongs?

An obvious advantage of living in a little country is that one may get to know it all. (As for disadvantages, there are none.) Giving myself a fairly severe examination with the map of Connecticut before me, I found that I had really got to know this manageable and man-sized territory rather well. I could remember where the best hickories grow, and the color of the soil on this ridge of granite or that slope of old red sandstone. I could tell where to look for laurel, for wild strawberries, or for columbines, in their seasons. For this I had not so much myself to thank as Connecticut, that she is little, so that a man can traverse her shortest boundary in two summer days. I thought that mighty Texas ought to know, and endless California to realize, that although Connecticut is indeed a tiny State, she feels the very opposite of shame for being so. I was glad that she had never made good her claim to the upper waters of the Susquehanna, and it did not distress me at all that Massachusetts and New York took from her long ago the little that they did — although I should by no means recommend that they try to do the same thing again.

Lovers of Connecticut would probably have said more than they have about her convenient size if it had not been for her deceptive completeness. We know that if the entire globe should suddenly shrink to one millionth of its present bulk, we should not feel any difference, because it would still be a fully furnished earth. Just so Connecticut is fully equipped as a State. She has farms and factories, mountains and seashore, multitude and solitude, the racing present and the lingering past. On a hill beside her great river a man can stand in the eighteenth century and look down on the towers of the twentieth. She is not at the expense of supporting any metropolis of her own, having had the canny and characteristic foresight to plant herself squarely between two great cities supported by her neighbors. If she had thought that a metropolis is really a good thing, doubtless she would have had one.

Sitting there in an apartment house of one of those two great cities with the map of my State before me, I thought not so much of her noble history or of the share she has in the world's work as of her wide and various beauty lying between the mountains and the sea on that day of midsummer sun. The green-gold map was a picture for me, or rather many pictures in one, and I read it as one reads a book. All down the central valley each mile was a mile of home. The names of towns and villages and hills and brooks along the river, from Enfield right to Saybrook, called up images as clear as those brought back by the names of my human friends. Whether they are beautiful names to others I cannot say, but to my ear they were like a chime of bells.

Just below Hartford I found the name of Wethersfield, one of the three oldest towns in the State, once a seaport from which sailing ships went out under clouds of canvas between the wide rich meadows on voyages round the Horn. Wethersfield, with its gigantic elm, its Christopher Wren spire, and its witch-haunted levels by the river, seemed to me on that August day, as I sat there in the din of Gotham's traffic, a haunt of ancient peace. Across the river lies Glastonbury with its romantic ravine and miles of peach orchard that light the hills with bloom in May. Farther down lies Portland of shipbuilding fame and mellow Middletown; and then come the Narrows, where the rocky hills crowd to the water's edge and the voyager sees nothing but forest boughs on either bank for mile after mile, hears only the knocking of little waves upon the rock or the song of the hermit thrush. Lower still are Higganum, Haddam, Middle Haddam, Hadlyme, Hamburg, and Old Lyme, each lovelier than the preceding and farther away from everything that seems to matter. And over them all is the spell of the river, widening here toward its journey's end in a majestic *rallentando*, with many a willowy island and sleeping cove. Long ago these towns played their little part in history. Now they dream and remember.

I thought how at Hadlyme, several Junes ago, a group of haymakers had called to me across three fields: 'Hallo, there! Come on over and help get in this grass before it rains.' I made some lame excuse about having to catch a train at Lyme, with which they were not satisfied. 'You'll find we're pretty good fellows over here,' one of them shouted, holding up something that looked like a large vinegar jug. I shouted back that I had not the slightest doubt of it, and tramped on down the road with half a sigh . . . and with more than half a curse for the whole curmudgeonly scheme of things that keeps us so timed by bells that we can seldom accept the kindliest offer of comradeship. Even now I count it among my lost opportunities that I did not jump the fence, help those five men with their last windrows, take supper with them as my wage, and sleep through the starry hours on their new-cut grass.

And I remembered Middle Haddam, most magical of all the river villages. Twilight has always been deepening into dusk when the boat has rounded to at her tiny pier, and I have never set foot in her streets. It may be that men go forth to their labors in Middle Haddam as they do in other towns and there may be gossip at the corner and marketing at the store, but to me it is a place where the lamps are always beginning to twinkle from leaf-screened windows, where the barn-doors are forever rumbling to for the night, and where the birds sing all year long their last crepuscular farewells. For me it is a place of pallid house-fronts under domes of leaves, with a pale steeple tapering up into the colored sky. Not more than a dozen houses are to be seen there, faintly lighted by the water still luminous in the afterglow. The steady sweep of the river lends a touch of solemnity to what might otherwise be only a graceful charm, and the hills ennoble it with seclusion. Shut off by wide water and by climbing woods, it rests like a pearl in a setting of green. Time never lands there. He comes down every evening on the river boat, stares for a few moments at the lights among the leaves, and then floats on. For he perfected Middle Haddam long ago, and will not touch it again.

When I had traveled in fancy all the way to Saybrook and the broad blue shining of the Sound, I began again far up to eastward, where higher hills crowd about the tributaries of the Willimantic, hiding villages of a wilder beauty. Here was tiny Union, where the deer are coming back and the red lynx walks again at noonday. Here were high white Tolland and Pomfret, the Willingtons gray and weather-beaten, ancient Andover, elmy Windham, and, farther south, historic Stonington and Mystic where the odor of whale-oil lingers yet.

Turning westward, I traced a wilder beauty still along the Housatonic, beginning at Salisbury in the high hills and coming down through Sharon, Canaan, Cornwall, Kent, New Milford, and Woodbury, each a painter's heaven. Close at hand were Winchester the forgotten, and Winsted, her flourishing child. Then came Litchfield, the worse for millionaires, and Thomaston, not improved by mills, and Plymouth, and Waterbury. With an eye roving over the map I picked out New Canaan, village of poets and friends; the Valley of the Silvermine, home of friends and of painters; Farmington the opulent, and Lebanon, once a scene of great affairs and still one of quiet loveliness. I looked out Hebron of Blue Law fame, and last, perhaps best of all in its silvery, ascetic way, little Gilead-on-the-Hill. And when I had got thus far I said very proudly to the United States of America assembled in imaginary conclave: 'By their fruits ye shall know them. Show me another State that has produced a village like Gilead.' There was no answer.

At about this point in my reverie I heard the fire engines scream down Amsterdam Avenue for the fourth or fifth time in an hour. Returning from my travels, I became aware of the city's thunder and wail all about me. A street-piano was grinding syncopated inanity round the bend of Morningside Drive; trolley-cars were lumbering down the hill and trucks were laboring up; a hundred klaxons were griding, a dozen newsboys were crying, a piano was playing in the adjoining apartment, and soon would begin the tyrannous reign of the radio. All at once it was revealed to me that I had had enough, at least for a time, of metropolitan sights and sounds and smells; that I could do very well if I did not hear that particular tune clattering up from the hurdy-gurdy for several weeks to come; that I could manage comfortably without the constant entertainment of the Fire Department; and, finally, that I could dispense for a while with the society of all those of my fellows who spend their eager days in collecting things such as dollars, fame, facts, and souls. For two months I had been able to see scarcely anything in the night sky except an idiotic dance of colored lights advertising chewing-gum; but in this revelation it came to me with a glow of fresh surprise that somewhere there must still be stars.

Then I said, taking up the little map of Connecticut to scan it once more in the gathering dusk: 'During these fifty weeks I have played, dubiously but hard, at the world's game, not sure that it is a good one; and now certainly I may step aside for the poor remainder of the year to see and to know and to do the things I love. I will go up into this land and possess it. And I will go up into it like a gentleman — which is to say on foot, staff in hand, with my few needments upon my back, taking no thought for the morrow, or for raiment, what I shall put on. I shall go where I like, and as fast as I like, or as slow, paying no attention to calendars and traveling as though railroads and automobiles had not been invented. If any man asks me to help him get in his hay, that will I gladly do. If any man cares to talk with me, I will not turn aside unless he be one who reads much and thinks little. I shall pause upon the things I really love, which are all very simple things and common. For two weeks I shall put the twentieth century in its place.'

Having made this resolve, I shortly after went to bed.

THE CALL

AND now comes in the sweet o' the year!
  The maple leaf is turning,
    Blue asters blazon the afternoon
    And on the edge of twilight, soon,
  The bonfires will be burning.

Innumerable goldenrod
  Invades our river-reaches;
    A million gentian-goblets burn
    Cerulean fire among the fern
  Beneath the pallid beeches.

A Spirit dances down the world
  On swift and shining sandals
    Who makes the woods rejoice and spills
    A splendor of flame upon the hills
  And lights the sumac candles.

Her clear voice calls my very name —
  Calls, and will have an answer;
    And all my heart is bound away
    Into the colored hills, to stray
  After that hidden dancer.

Farewell to friend and wife and child
  And all things wise or sober!

I have drunk deep of vivid stains
And feel like magic in my veins
The wild wine of October.

Lead on, dear golden tattered paths
Rustling with summer plunder.
My foot is light, my heart is strong
To follow this beguiling song
That cries and croons and calls along
The winding road to wonder.

II

FRIENDSHIP VALLEY

*Give me the clear blue sky over my head, and the green turf beneath
my feet, a winding road before me, and a three hours' march to
dinner — and then to thinking!*

— HAZLITT

 SOME weeks later, at three o'clock in
the afternoon of a September day,
I put in my plough where Israel Putnam left his, at the little town of
Brooklyn, which looks out over the
Quinebaug Valley toward the blue
hills of Rhode Island. Here I stepped
at once out of the twentieth century into Connecticut.
Those who are likely to read such a book as this will
not need to be told that Connecticut, and indeed New
England as a whole, is bounded by years as well as
by lines on the map. No part of it extends into our
time, and only here and there, in districts sheltered
from the winds of modernity, does it extend to the
Civil War.

Brooklyn lies far away on the other side of that distant epoch. Most of its houses are very old, and so are
too many of the people. Elderly ladies were sitting on
the deep piazzas, their white hair parted in the middle
over serene brows, waiting alone — or so I liked to
fancy — for the latest news of the Continental Army.

The elm trees towering over the small white houses were old and gray. On the green, where asters and goldenrod flourished undisturbed, stands the church of the 'First Ecclesiastical Society of Brooklyn,' erected under the leadership of Colonel Israel Putnam in 1771 — a respectable age for a church edifice in this region. Yet I should hesitate to call the town really old. Rather, it has been ripened, and perhaps a little tarnished, by time. There hangs about it just a suggestion of mildew, as on a beautiful apple that has clung too long to the bough.

The village would have been very quiet on that drowsy afternoon if it had not been for the whine of three or four rusted windmills, the multiloquence of a thousand white leghorns, and the shrill of a million crickets. The people made no noise. Such few of them as I saw seemed to be plunged in meditation, and I judged from the memorial tablets here and there that they were probably thinking about Israel Putnam. For the fame of this local hero bestrides the village — in which he was once bell-ringer and care-taker of the church at a salary of three pounds a year — like a Colossus. And strange it is to ponder how that fame now rests hardly at all upon his numerous and valuable services in the French-and-Indian War, during the Conspiracy of Pontiac, and on many a field of the Revolution, but almost entirely upon three spectacular acts that have caught the popular fancy: his descent into the wolf-den and slaying of the huge she-wolf of Pomfret, his leaving the plough in the furrow like Cin-

cinnatus of old when he heard the news from Lexington and Concord, and his daring downhill ride at Stamford — this last exploit showing that he could look

heroic even when running away.   Beside these events his solid work as an able and industrious soldier has shrunk into insignificance.   Clio, as Oscar Wilde pointed out, is the least serious of the Muses, and Fame strikes as capriciously as lightning. Nathan Hale secured his, although he had won it otherwise, by an epigram. But perhaps the popular imagination is right, after all, in concentrating upon these three moments of Putnam's life: it may be that they sum him up. Observe also that whereas his real work was done in Massachusetts, New York State, and in far-off Detroit, these three remembered deeds were all performed in Connecticut.

Most of the people who live in Brooklyn to-day are of English origin. As I went out of the village I met a man mowing grass with a scythe who showed beyond doubt, in a few sentences, that he was of pure Yankee descent. I asked him, with a glance at the ominous clouds rolling up from the southeast, whether he thought it would rain.

'Prob'ly will,' said he, 'see's I've just begun to mow.'

Then he looked critically at the clouds for a moment, spat on the whetstone poised in his hand, and remarked: 'But it don't really seem like we'd have a rain. I guess it might *shower* a bit, though.'

'You make a fine distinction,' I said, 'between showers and rain.'

'Wall, yes, *I* do; but if a man's walking out in it like you be, one wets him through 'baout as quick as t'other.'

'Zing, zing, zing,' went the whetstone along the scythe-blade, preventing further conversation. In this philosopher's cheerful expectation of the worst I found one of the major traits of the true Yankee. He inherited this ignoble wisdom from a long line of Christian Stoics who habitually regarded the present world as a 'vale of tears.' Looking back through the centuries as far as history lights the way, we do not find a time when the forbears of the Connecticut Yankee enjoyed any wide margins of security. In Old England they belonged for the most part to the submerged classes, precariously clinging to spare livelihoods, and in the new land it has still seemed wiser to expect disaster than prosperity. What wonder that the Yankee of to-day tends to look for the worst and to take even his pleasures somewhat sadly?

I had not gone two hundred yards from the village green along the road that leads from Brooklyn to Pomfret when I came to a sign-board swinging from an elm tree with this heartening legend painted on it in bold lettering:

FRIENDSHIP VALLEY

How far that valley was supposed to extend there was nothing to indicate, and I did not find it marked in my Government Survey map, which is drawn to the scale of an inch to the mile. Only little by little and day by day, as my walk went on, did I discover how remarkably extensive this vale of friends, into which I had the good luck to strike in the first hour of my journey, really is. I traced it that afternoon straight up the hill to Pomfret, a matter of ten miles. There I got directions enabling me to follow it on into Fairford, whence it runs uphill again into Union and then down to Stafford. To make a long but pleasant story short, I discovered during the next two weeks that Friendship Valley rambles right across the northern boundary of Connecticut and down the western at least as far as the town of Kent, in defiance of all geographical orthodoxy, crossing many a stream and watershed on its way. Of course I could not know at the time what a discovery I had made; but I had the sense to take the sign-board as a good omen, and went up the hill with a lighter heart.

All roads that aspire to go to Pomfret must go uphill, and this road of mine lost no time in beginning. My pack and I, not yet well acquainted, had a few minor adjustments to make almost at once — and then, on and up. There were stately old houses behind old and stately elms on either side of the path, and I was glad to think that they must all be full of friends even though I had not time to stop and call. The long, sloping fields into which I looked over the stone wall were prosperous with cattle, and strangely similar, I thought, to some of the tamer hillsides in the English Lake Country. Scarcely had this notion crossed my mind, however, when three dogs dashed wildly at me out of a dooryard and pursued me for a long way with every species of canine profanity and vituperation, dispelling at once the illusion that I was in the land of Wordsworth. English dogs are better bred.

Of course it is profoundly unwise to make any sweeping declaration of one's general attitude toward dogs, either for or against, just as it is social suicide to say that one does or does not believe in Prohibition. Half the people who read or hear your ill-advised remarks will say to themselves, 'So he is *that* sort of person!'  and will leave you thereafter severely alone. Yet I will make bold to say that I am not fond of the dog that follows me down the public highway with snarls and curses when I have done nothing whatever, unless by merely existing, to earn his displeasure. A dog that confines his paroxysms to the limits of his own yard and makes ready to tear your throat the instant you pass the gate is at least minding his own business, although his manners leave something to be desired. Less than this can be said for the three that ran after me in the Valley of Friendship — a name that seemed for the moment almost ironical. And something far less still is to be said for the hounds of hell that run silently up behind the pedestrian long after he has passed their domain and make their presence known by a terrifying bay when they are upon him.

Such as these, I know, are one in ten thousand, but that is more than enough. One of them I encountered long ago, after dark, on a hill in southern New Hampshire. His master's house, when I passed it, had been utterly silent, with not a creature stirring. I had walked on for perhaps an eighth of a mile under heavy trees that left me only light enough to see the path when I heard a swift thud of heavy but muffled feet behind me, and at almost the same instant the yell of a hound in sight of its prey. My walking-stick swung round on the pivot of my body, as I turned to face him, and descended with all the force I could muster. It cut the empty air. What had been the front elevation of a dog that looked to me about the size of a well-grown horse — I speak not of the  probable fact but of the actual seeming — was suddenly transformed into the rear. He went away from there as swiftly and silently as he had come. I do not know why he ran after me in that blood-curdling fashion, and I have still less idea why he ran away from a stick that should have been no more frightening to him than a mere trout-rod, but I do know that I am not fond of that kind of dog. All the Rabs and Beautiful Joes in the world will not abate a jot of my confident hope that he is at this moment doing duty at the gates of hell in place of Cerberus.

Dogs, I admit, like human beings, are of several different sorts. A rough classification, convenient for wayfaring men, is that which divides them into big, little, and middling; for it is to be observed that the big dog could if he would, and that the little dog would if he could, but that only the middle-sized dog, in whom ability and inclination meet, requires close attention. If the mastiff were as ferocious as the black-and-tan, either he or we would have to move out. Fortunately, the law of compensation works here, as elsewhere. I remember being pursued down the road one day by a scrap of canine valor hardly more than a foot in length, and no sooner had he left off his imprecations at my retreating heels than I came to a majestic Great Dane standing squarely between the posts of his front gate. He merely stood there and looked at me without a word as I went by, and his look seemed faintly contemptuous. There was not a quiver in his mighty muscles. I judged that he must dine on steaks of dinosaur, for a mere man was to him a negligible morsel.

Another classification soon learned by gentlemen of the road is that which distinguishes sharply between dogs at home and dogs *en route*. I have often struck up acquaintance with a dog off duty, enjoying his leisure in the woods or lanes, and we have gone along together for a mile or so conversing in the most amicable way; yet this same animal, so courteous and affable as a companion, if he were to see me trudging by his houseplace with pack and stick, would have nothing for me but scurrilous language. That fundamental article of our real religion which we are pleased to call the 'rights of private property' is best studied, in all its beauty and charm, in the frenzied vociferation of a cur left in charge of a country shack, protesting against your trespass as though he owned a First Folio Shakespeare or a trout stream, or had just bribed a government official for the exclusive rights in oil.

Those who think this too severe an indictment should remember that it is written by a walking man. Now it is generally agreed in these days, among dogs and their masters alike, that a walker is either very eccentric or else very poor, and they agree also that the one condition is about as bad as the other. They resent eccentricity because it  puts them to the trouble of remembering superfluous smells. They like to have all men fit readily into the recognized pigeon-holes, such as that for business men, that for professional men, and . . . I think there are no others. As for the walker's probable poverty, they agree with Tennyson's Northern Farmer that 'the poor in the lump is bad.' And so it makes a great difference in one's reception by country dogs whether one goes by them in an automobile or on foot. A large proportion of those that I have met in my rural travels have been incorrigible snobs. King Lear discovered the same thing. Never in his long life, apparently, had he been barked at until he put off his splendor and was thrust forth in the storm upon the heath; then came his pathetic ejaculation of astonishment:

> The little dogs and all,
> Tray, Blanche, and Sweetheart, see, they bark at me!

We should, of course, take the opinion about dogs of

the fine lady who rides along the avenue with her prize poodle on her lap, but we should also take the opinion of the tramp who limps down the country lane in 'looped and windowed raggedness.'

However, this is enough. There is something grotesque, after all, in accusations of snobbishness and insolence in office leveled by a member of the human species against dogs. The worst that we can say of them is that they remind us sometimes too vividly of ourselves.

At the top of the hill above Brooklyn there is a tiny white schoolhouse hidden behind boulders almost as large as itself and shaded by pine trees. Here I rested  for a moment, listening to the now retreating threats of my three pursuers and looking out over the townships to the south and east. The gloomy prognostications of the man with the scythe seemed unlikely to be fulfilled. All the sky-chambers were being swept and burnished into that crystalline purity best seen, I think, in Connecticut on a September day. Church towers ten miles off across the valley shone vividly in the late sunshine, recalling Tennyson's audacious hyperbole:

Sown in a wrinkle of the monstrous hill
The city sparkles like a grain of salt.

A few rods beyond the schoolhouse I came to a wide
common running straight along the ridge of the hill
toward Pomfret Street. Mile after mile it ran between
grassy borders rich with aster and goldenrod. Whenever I could look out at the farther hills between the
apple boughs tossing in the wind, I saw that the colors
were deepening upon them and that the cold clearness
of the sky increased as the sun declined. Light and
hue swept up in a vivid crescendo before the final
chords of the afterglow and the coda of the stars.
Although I was expected in Pomfret and had three
miles to go in forty minutes, I paused to see the last
flicker of sunlight on the vane of the highest church
spire in the valley.

SUNDOWN

FAR out across the quiet afternoon
The ridges wrinkle eastward to the sea —
Vast granite surges rolling silently
Between the setting sun and rising moon
And breaking, far away, without a sound,
In dim blue foam on the horizon's round.

Over their taciturn
Cold majesty the clouds still glow and burn;
But deeper, where the river-willows lean,
Dim companies of the dusk convene
And creep and grope
Along the lower slope,
And blur with gradual shadow tree by tree.
And now they overflow and drown
The first low valley town —
Save where some farmhouse window hoards a gleam,
Or some tall weather-vane
Or tapered spire shines in a special beam,
Like the last vague reluctant dream
Of childhood in a dying brain.

Slowly, above the lake and little ponds,
The long lights change to bronze;
Yet in the elm-tops of the highest hill
Some glimmer lingers still.

It fades to rose,
It dims, it dies, and goes
Farther than thought can follow. . . . The last ray
That lit, one moment since, our village spire,
And burnished every weather-cock with fire,
Is out among the climbing stars at play.

So ends another day
Its lingering and leisurely farewell,
While through the windings of some hidden dell
The last faint drowsy cowbell thins away.

III
ROUND THE CORNER OF TIME

It is indeed the unseen, the imagined, the untold-of, the fabulous, the forgotten, that alone lies safe from mortal moth and rust.
— WALTER DE LA MARE

I CANNOT quite decide why it is that I have so little to say about Pomfret, which, as every one ought to know, is one of the most beautiful towns in the world. Certainly it makes a vivid impression, though not one that is easily described. I remember the mighty ridge on which it stands, its avenue of elms, the long line of its matronly maples with branches sweeping the grass, the ample inn, and the hills that roll away from it like gigantic billows toward the sea. I remember its homes, and one of them in particular with enduring pleasure. I remember the school once attended by Whistler, and I like to think that he learned in this Connecticut town some secrets of his spare and ascetic art. But these are all mental pictures, and the essence of Pomfret lies rather in its 'atmosphere,' for which there are no words. It should be easier to phrase the town in music than in prose discourse. Indeed, I find that I remem-

ber Pomfret best in terms of sound, and of quiet . . .
for the quietness of one place differs widely from that
of another, and the quiet of Pomfret is its true voice.
In the woods of Venily — a 'plot of beechen green and
shadows numberless' on the slope of Pomfret hill —
the stillness that broods over the whole township is
brought to a focus and becomes expectant, prophetic,
pregnant with significance. Perhaps, therefore, I can
say most clearly what the town means to me by setting
down here an unrhymed sonnet I had written in the
train some weeks before, after a visit to those magic
woods:

> The silvery and fragile horns of silence
> Are blown among the hills of Venily,
> Uplifted in the Kingdoms of Enchantment
> To hallow all the chambers of the air.
> 'What means this secret singing?' aspen whispers
> Softly to river-reed. 'I know not, yet.'
> Over that delicate fanfare of far-off music
> The giant oak has mused two hundred years.
>
> But such mysterious reveille must herald
> Some vast and inconceivable event.
> There is a breathless stir of preparation
> Among the boughs, and rumor in the hills.
> The forest listens. By her shadowy water
> The Naiad waits, a finger at her lip.

On the morning after my arrival at Pomfret, I set
forth, conducted by the Poet and Painter of Venily,
toward the Village of Voices, of which I had long known
the fame. As this is a secret place, I must not divulge
our route, and I shall only say that after going downhill,

uphill, down again and up, for how many miles I have no recollection, we came to the Old Burying Ground.

There were some thirty graves in the small enclosure, surrounded by a wall of rough field stone. Several of the tablets had been tilted, snapped, or thrown down

by the trees that had invaded the sanctuary. Nothing could symbolize the insolent trampling of life upon death, of the present upon the past, more vividly than the way in which these robust oaks and maples made free with God's acre, elbowing the tombstones aside, splitting coffins, riving skulls, and drawing their sustenance from what had once been human. For the first time in my life I felt indignant at trees, and I told the Poet that I thought it would have been decent of them to have left us these few square feet, seeing that they had unnumbered square miles all about; but he said that they were merely taking back their own. The little graveyard had been so long neglected that several chance-sown trees had grown to maturity there and had fallen across the mounds, mingling their substance with the common mould. Clearly, this was no place to nourish jealousies against the vegetable kingdom, for the doom of all its subjects was indistinguishable from ours. Trees and men were descending together there into the democracy of the dust.

The graveyards of New England can be gay or sad, humorous or severe, bleak or beautiful, but they are always intensely interesting. The spiritual history of our first two hundred years is nowhere written down more clearly than in these slate and granite pages of the hillside, these neglected Americana of the open air. For years I have studied the headstones of Connecticut with camera and pencil and tracing-paper, more and more amazed at their crude power and occasional beauty, more and more convinced that in our neglect of them we have ignored the most significant record that the Puritans left. If it were not for fear of importing the methods of a doctoral dissertation into a holiday book I should set down here some of the results of my researches in these libraries of stone. I could show, if this were the right time and place, how the Calvinists of America were slowly drawn away from thoughts of death and hell merely by tracing the stages of gradual mollification through which the original death's-head or *Memento Mori* of their headstones passed successively into the Winged Skull, the Cherub with Two Mouths, the Cherub Proper, the Portrait, and, finally, the Urn and Cypress. . . . But that would be mere scholarship, and this is a book of moods and whims.

Much more to my present purpose was that slow but steady and sure intermingling of men and trees in the graveyard above the Village of Voices. A thousand years from now the subtlest chemistry will not tell them apart, or give any clue as to which grain of dust once floated high in the summer air and which was once instinct with human thought and passion. Even the headstones will soon be gone, for the earth climbs swiftly about them. I have seen stones that once stood four feet above the ground showing no more than as many inches. For Nature is not fond of these memorials of man's grief, and she sets to work upon them as soon as they are exposed to her power, never abandoning the attack until she has torn them to bits or covered them quite over. An active imagination, observing how they sink a little every year, might suggest that the dead are pulling them down out of sight, ashamed of the inscriptions they bear.

In one of W. H. Hudson's books there is an oddly characteristic passage about the red and golden algæ that glorify the older tombstones of southern England. Tombstones, to Hudson, are nothing but natural objects, and he is quite indifferent to the human drama, ranging from farce to high tragedy, that they represent. His passion for life, even in its lowest forms, carries him here into the very sanctuary of death itself. Although he does not say so, I think that what delights him in these gay algæ is to see Nature taking back her own, erasing the scars of our alien sorrow — to see life still triumphant, and the tides of life already splashing upon and threatening to overwhelm the emblems of death. The threat will soon be carried out.

The path that goes down from the Old Burying Ground to the Village of Voices is devious and blurred and hard to find; but we came at last to a little brook of brown-black water with glints and whorls of golden light deep down in it, and soon after to a grove of hemlocks. Here was once a hamlet of Welsh people who ran a small factory for the making of spindles, the ruins of which are still to be seen farther down the brook. Here had been their houses, represented to-day by a few gaping cellar-holes out of which tall trees are growing; but here *is* the Village of Voices. For the place is peopled still, like Prospero's Isle, by 'sounds and sweet airs that give delight and hurt not.' Although there is now no human habitation for a long distance round about and no one goes there except the few who go to listen, yet there is always a hum and stir of human life, the Poet and Painter tell me, in the Village. They hear the laughter of children at play in dooryards where the vixen litters now amid an impenetrable thicket. They hear the voices of mothers who have long been dust calling their children into the homes that are now mere holes in the earth. They hear vague snatches of song, and a hum of harp-strings in

the air, and the rumble of heavy wagons along an obliterated road. It is as though sounds were able in this place to get round that incomprehensible corner, to pierce that mysterious sound-proof wall, that we call Time. A reader of Ouspensky's 'Tertium Organum' might be tempted to say that the voices somehow break through from the fourth dimension into our poorer world of three.

I am aware that I shall seem to be talking nonsense, and if any incredulous person will come forward with a really intelligible statement of what time is I shall be glad to retract all the little that I have implied. (Saint Augustine it was, I think, who said: 'If you ask me what Time is, I know not; but if you ask me not, I know.') In the meanwhile I shall continue to think it less strange that the voices of the past win through to mortal ears now and then in the Village of Voices than it is that they are silent to us always in almost every other place. The well-nigh universal cessation and not the exceptional continuance is what I wonder at, stubbornly, never quite convinced, because I find it essentially incredible. Every one must have felt, with Abt Vogler, while listening to the gradual building of some intricate structure of sound, that it ought to be, that it must be, at least as enduring as temples of stone. How can we believe that even the rock-hewn buildings of Bach fade instantly away, like fireworks against the night sky? I choose to fancy that they are saved somewhere, that they are safe eternally, and that this fearful figure of Time who seems to lay his muting finger upon the strings of all our music is only a specter of our own conjuring. Thinking, or rather feeling, in this way, I often amuse myself with the notion of a great reservoir of tone into which all the beautiful and beloved voices of the past have sunk down, and where they now lie asleep, awaiting some unimaginable reveille.

Clambering about the old cellar-holes, we saw that the people who had lived here had been skilful and honest builders. A hundred years had not tilted their chimneys or shaken the Cyclopean masonry of their foundations. Fire and vegetation and damp had eaten all but the stones they laid, but these, we thought, would remain to report well of them for a thousand years to come. Evidently they were strong men and women who lived here, and such as take strong hold on life, striking deep roots into the earth. The Poet and Painter told me that the Voices were always happy ... an important bit of corroborative evidence. The greater number of the ghosts one hears about are unbelievable because there is really no reason why a sad and disconsolate spirit should return to the scene of its misery. People who have been happy while they were here make the most credible *revenants*. Let us suppose that the villagers who once made this hillside ring with laughter and song were a joyous, vigorous, full-blooded lot, lovers of life, lovers of earth. Sitting there in the sunshine on one of their worn doorsills, I found it easier to suppose that such people would come back than to think they would not. The people in the little burying ground above had seemed to me utterly dead and gone forever. What made the difference? Well, perhaps we are given after death not the things we have 'deserved' but those we have most deeply desired — unless desire be itself a kind of deserving. In that case, all those who have blasphemed God's world by regarding it as a mere vestibule to their tinsel-and-gingerbread heaven may be invited to stay away, and only the ghosts of the happy shall inherit the earth. Now the people in the burial ground were Puritans, but those of the Village of Voices were Welsh.

When we came to the Village all the voices were silent, and only the breeze in the hemlocks and the song of the stream below broke the forest hush. We waited there a few minutes, and then the Poet took me down the brook to bathe in Dancing Rock Pool while the Painter set to work with colored crayons upon a sketch of the hemlocks. The water in the pool was black with leaf-mould, so that our bodies glimmered in it like old ivory, and it was as cold as a drop just fallen from a gigantic icicle; but all this, and even the boulders on every hand that made it impossible to take more than a stroke or two, did not spoil the pleasure of bathing in such a place.

The Painter told us upon our return that the Voices had come in a rush half an hour after we left, and then had died down. They did not come back again during our stay. Not to have heard them leaves in the world for me one aspiration the more.

'MUSIC WHEN SOFT VOICES DIE'

Silence will have her own . . .
Every wandering tone:
All of the lisping speech
Of aspen tree and of beech,
All the pine said to the oak,
All that the snow-flake spoke
To the ground.
Voices dwindle and sink
Over the moment's brink
As a fountain falls, or a flame.
They hear an imperious call
From the country whence they came,
And suddenly flutter and fall
Like the leaves of a frost-bitten tree.
Ah, mystery!
Every ghost of a sound
Must drop from the loneliest hill
And sleep, and be still.

Wearily, one by one,
They fall from the wind and the sun
To a pool at the earth's dark roots.
There throbs and thins
The song of forgotten violins
And every note of the smooth long silver flutes
Old poets played
In the wavering green of Sicilian shade.

And Helen's voice is there,
And the cry of Sappho's lyre
Crowding the weight of a world's despair
Upon one passionate wire.
Hid in that soundless dark
Is the song of Shelley's lark
And the voice of a dim immortal bird
Catullus heard
Charming the moonlit surf of Sirmio
One midnight long ago.

This is the sorrowful doom
That makes of all music a sighing,
Only a march to the tomb,
A farewell, a beautiful dying.
Oceans of quiet surround
Each islet of fragile sound,
Where the pomp of the trumpet is drowned
And the hautboy's tremulous crying.
Into that quietness comes
All the troubling of turbulent drums,
And the best-loved voice lies alone
In that place of no replying. . . .

Silence will have her own.

GRAVEYARD SUITE

I. ETIQUETTE IN GOD'S ACRE

In a drowsy New England graveyard, two headstones face each other beneath an ancient pine tree. One, erected in 1924, is of fresh-hewn granite. It catches the long, dusty rays that sift through the pine branches upon a surface polished to a brilliant gloss. Carefully tended grass struggles up between the pine needles about it, and a wreath of artificial flowers lies at its base. The other, dated 1779, is of rudely chiselled slate and bears a shallow, almost illegible inscription in verse. It seems on the point of falling, and is supported chiefly by the pine needles that have climbed to half its height. A chipmunk has burrowed beneath it.

Granite Headstone (jauntily)
  You there with the moss,
  You doddering old slate one,
  Sun-bleached, bird-spotted, weather-worn, —
  Will you lean just a bit to the *other* side?
  I've waited two years, now,
  Expecting your never-too-much-to-be-lamented
        demise
  Any day.
  If you really think you must fall,
  Pray don't delay it on my account.
  The fact is, you shut off my view.

Slate Headstone (as though to itself)
  Either the sexton dotes or earth has grown
  Too full of graves to shelter all its dead —

No grain of dust, at last, but it has breathed
And walked.   Yearly these smooth young parvenus
Intrude and jostle and crowd us to the wall.

Granite Headstone (puzzled)
What's this he's mumbling about 'parvenus'?
Does he mean me?
Anyhow, it sounds abusive;
And he talks in blank verse, too.
Hello, you funny old washed-out blue one!
Is it Shakespeare you've got over there,
Or the fellow that wrote the Elegy?
I dare say, now, you never heard of Spoon River.

Slate Headstone (after a few hours of thought)
I never heard its dull cacophanous name.
The Lethe is the only stream I know.

Granite Headstone (affably)
Well, anyhow,
There's our precedent for sepulchral loquacity.
Speaking of that, though, how the times change!
Take the fashions in headstones, now.
Somebody's going to dig you up for a curio one of
        these days,
Take it from me. . . .
You're a scream, with your stiff old weeping-
        willow —
Or is it a death's head?
The birds have made it hard to tell which.

And then take the funny old rhymes
There at your waistband . . .
Hour — bow'r — show'r — flow'r,
And something, I suppose, about meeting in heaven.
Quite quaint, I call it.

But say, listen here;
Who cares about you?
How long since your weeds were cut?
How long since anybody scraped away the leaves
To see how old you are?
How long since anybody left a wreath for you?
In short,
Why not fall down and be done with it?

Slate Headstone (going in to finish off)
Once you were pure with mountain wind and rain,
Unsullied by the taint of mortal grief;
But now the winds of many a winter night
And many an April rain must cleanse away
The fresh defilement of a human touch.
Ten thousand suns must shine, ten thousand dews
Wash you with lustral waters, and the wreck
Of many a withered June must cover you
Under a surge of drifting sibilant gold
Before the sky shall find you clean again.

But the forgetful years are very kind.
Last summer roses grew beside you there.
Now they are paper. Soon there will be none.

The climbing mould and moss and the creeping weed
Will dull your shameful freshness year by year;
Weather will gnaw with a tireless tooth, the thing
You hide will crumble down to cleanly dust,
Till the earth has wholly taken back her own.

When you are dearer to the jay and crow
Than unto any grieving human heart,
And when the fire-fly and the bat and mole
Have given you back their ancient fellowship,
When there is left for you no thought or tear,
Only the clinging moss and the friendly weed,
When you are one in human memory
With any rain-washed boulder of the hill,
Then you and I may meet in equal talk.

Meantime, those of us that are oldest here
Make it a custom not to recognize
Those who are dead less than a hundred years.

Granite Headstone (visibly impressed)
    O! Indeed!

The slate headstone fixes its gaze upon a remote
point in space and serenely ignores its neighbor for a
full century.

II. A PAGE FROM THE DEVIL'S JEST BOOK

Deacon Brown for thirty years
Kept his wife in sighs and tears,
And she in turn tormented him
With rancor till her eyes were dim;
Until at last, both wearied out
With blow and buffet, scream and shout,
Since neither would give up the fight,
They died together, out of spite.

Folk said: 'It will not do to say,
On stone that lasts till Judgment Day
The truth of how they lived and died.'
And so those pious people lied.
They crowned the gravestone with a wreath
And carved two clasped hands underneath,
With rhymes that told how gentle, true,
And loving they had been — those two!

And that is all the village knows . . .
But even now a rumor goes
That often, deep at night, a fiend
Slips through the moony meadow screened
By shifting leaves, and in the weeds
Beside the headstone sits and reads
With huge delight those epitaphs,
And laughs and laughs — Lord, how he laughs!

III. WEDLOCK

Said Flesh to Bone: 'This many a year
We've kept the road together, dear;
Now there's a thing I'd like to say
Frankly, as an old friend may.
Since we began, we two have seen
Sorrow and joy and all between,
Despair and love and bitter fight,
Stars burning in the frosty night,
Cities of men, the hills, the sea. . . .
Nothing too far for you and me!
But now — it grieves me to the heart
To ask it — have you done your part?
Often at night I'm quite worn out
Just with bearing you about.
Often it's all that I can do
Just to lift and carry you —
To get you up and ride you round
And keep you moving on the ground.
And year by year I think you grow
Heavier, more dull, more slow,
Like an old machine that grinds and clicks,
A bag of sockets, hoops, and sticks.
I want to run, I want to soar,
But you lie heavy at the core
So that I only seem to creep
Feebly toward some final sleep.'

Said Bone to Flesh: 'I always knew

There'd be no use in telling you.
Why should you think it such a boon
For me to dance to your crazy tune,
Jerked by tendons, pulled by strings?
And now you talk of wanting wings!
The attitudes you put me through,
The frantic things you make me do,
If he could see them in a dream,
Would make a brazen monkey scream.
However, take your own good time.
It's tedious for me now, but I'm
Thinking soon to lay me down
In some still granite-gated town,
Some city of my kith and kin,
Where, though you may just enter in,
However hale, however strong,
You will not care to tarry long.
I'll be the winner in the end,
So take your time and pleasure, friend.'

IV. METEMPSYCHOSIS

On either side the dead men lay,
  Each with his lettered stone,
All deaf and blind and clogged with clay,
  While I strode on alone.

The morning had no song, no word
  For those dull sleepers now,
And oh! they could not hear the bird
  That warbled from the bough.

They could not feel the wind go by,
  Nor see the elm trees bowed
Before the wind against a sky
  Deepened by fleets of cloud.

But suddenly along my veins
  I felt the strength of ten.
Old loves and lusts and deathless pains
  Of all those buried men,

Old dreams and unassuaged desires,
  Death-frosted in the bud,
Swept through me, and long-sleeping fires
  Woke riot in my blood.

I laughed, I sang, I clasped a tree,
　I gulped the air, I drew
The breath of heaven into me,
　I drank the morning's blue.

Then all at once down the long hill
　My feet began to run
For love of those that lay so still
　And could not feel the sun.

IV

SUNSHINE AND SHADOW

M'aimeroy mieulx deuxiesme ou troisiesme à Perigueux que premier à Paris.

— MONTAIGNE

 To give exact directions for going from the Village of Voices to the town of Fairford would not be playing fair with the Painter and the Poet, because those directions might easily be followed in reverse order, and I shall content myself with saying, therefore, that the road I walked that afternoon ran all the way through pure and uncontaminated Connecticut. In that northwest corner of Windham County the slopes are long, clean, and sweeping; the hills are nobly sculptured. Men and Nature have collaborated more amicably there, to a more harmonious result, than they have elsewhere, and it is a joy to trace from every hilltop the fused and intermingling shares of each. In America, for the most part, we have either gashed and blistered the country we have touched, leaving it to bleed with wounds that only centuries can heal, or else we have man-handled it into 'estates' that are often worse than desolation. Our dealing with this fair land has been a gigantic rape committed by greed upon beauty, so

that a civilized foreigner, judging us by the trail we
have left, might write down on the map, in huge capi-
tal letters extending from Mexico into Maine, the one
word BARBARIA. Yet here and there one comes upon
little stretches of country where men have lived on the
land as though they loved it, and where the land,
therefore, has dealt lovingly with them. It was such a
country that I walked through on the way to Fairford.

First I climbed a long slope where the voice of the
silage-chopper was loud in the land, coughing and
stuttering so as to shake the air from hill to hill, and
near the top I came to a group of farm-hands who were
feeding one of these raucous machines with corn. One
lifted the bladed stalks from the wagon and laid them,
stems foremost, in the wooden trestle. Immediately
they began to move, with a violent trembling, toward
the knives, while a second butcher laid them out for
their death with a few swift pushes and pulls. I could
see how their trembling increased as they neared the
whirring edges, and when the blades bit into the thick
woody stalks I could hear above the engine's roar a
faint expiring scream. One week before they had been
beautiful on the hillside in their whispering ranks —
fifteen feet tall, for this had been a good corn year.
Now they were being chopped into sticky cylinders
and hoisted into a silo, there to be embalmed and await
the maws of cattle. Inevitably my sympathies were
with the corn, for it seemed alive and sentient. There
came to mind Carmen Sylva's poem in which the new-
made hay speaks:

Yesterday's flowers am I,
And I have drunk my last sweet draught of dew.
Young maidens came and sang me to my death . . .

The corn, I thought, was dying to a sterner music.

Before long, however, I realized that it would be well to set a decent limit to this fantastic sentimental-ism. Three hours before I had been indignant at oaks and maples for crowding the human dead in a for-gotten graveyard, and now I was espousing the cause of vegetables against my own kind. I saw that the farm-ers, like the trees, were only 'taking back their own.' The violent butchery of the corn, pleasantly painful as it was for an idle man on the quest of sensation to witness, was only a trivial incident in the monotonous process by which matter is churned eternally from life into death and back again. This process, which goes on as well in gardens as in graveyards and almost as obviously in restaurants as in silage-choppers, might be a pitiful thing in its total cosmic aspect, as the thinkers of the East have always held it to be; but a rambler in the western world need not concern himself about that. If I must sympathize at all, why not with the real glee of the farmers rather than with the corn's imagined woe? They were enjoying the stertorous din of the engine over which their voices could not be heard in the loudest shout, so that they had to communicate by gestures. This was harvest-home for them, the shining goal of their year. After I had taken the road again the voice of the engine followed me for miles as their song of rejoicing, the best substitute Christian

Connecticut has for the joyous ceremonies with which the pagans once brought home their sheaves and wine-skins.

Certainly it is a main defect in Connecticut agriculture — and in this respect Connecticut may stand for most of America — that it rests upon none but Christian, or perhaps it would be better to say none but Puritan, traditions. This means that the toil is left without the joy, the business without the beauty. That bigoted fear of pagan ceremonial which made the early Puritans blaspheme even Christmas has been, perhaps, the most potent among the several influences that have made the New England farmer's life comparatively dull, converting the most dignified of human occupations into a toilsome and prosaic way of making an uncertain living. Whatever else may be said for the Calvinists of New England, they had little instinct for gaiety. If happiness be the supreme test of human beings, as I believe it is, then they were flat failures. They cut us off from our past, destroyed some of our most precious racial memories, and, worst of all, severed us from the earth. This may suggest a reason why the American farmer is so often ashamed of his work while the English farmer is proudly and passionately fond of his, loving every inch of his land and treating it like a lover. An English countryman asks nothing better than to live and die on his patrimonial acres, or in the village where he was born — and I have thought that I could explain this 'patriotism of the steeple,' which we so clearly lack and greatly need,

while watching the men of a Devonshire parish turn
the hard labor of sheep-shearing into a fortnight's
festival by means of old Use and Wont and a plentiful
supply of beer.

The plaint of the farmer has been heard, no doubt,
ever since men began to live on the edible grasses, but
in America his most legitimate complaint has hitherto
been that his life is lonely and bleak and dull. I am
not sure that the radio, the telephone, and the automobile will ultimately enliven it very much, for these
things bring him chiefly the dullness of the city, pro-
viding a choice between one tedium and another. His
means of happiness lie nearer at hand, but he must be
taught to use them, as a man whose memory has been
shattered by a blow must be taught to use knife and
fork. If I were an American Secretary of Agriculture
I should try to steal some time from the study of fer-
tilizers and rotation of crops to consider the songs that
ploughboys and sowers and shepherds and hedgers
used to sing as they went about their work. I should
want to know about the agricultural feasts that once
marked off the seasons of the year, and I should read
all that I could find about Harvest-Home, Blessing
the Fields, Parochial Perambulations, Wake Days, the
Hock-Cart, the Ploughman's Feast, Sword Dances,
Mummings, May Poles, Fool Ploughs, Yuletide, and
Midsummer Eve. I should send over to the Library
of Congress for Thomas Tusser's 'Hundreth Good
Pointes of Husbandry' and for Gervase Markham on
the Gentleman Farmer, not forgetting the poems of

Robert Herrick and William Browne and John Clare. Eventually, I might decide to import a few selected superstitions.

At the top of a gradual slope I came to a road running northward along a ridge, and the borders of it were woven close to left and right by a thicket of young birches, maples, and aspens. The leaves, already yellowing, were all atwinkle in the northwest wind, so that the lane before me was one vista of dazzle and shine. Tall grass grew between the wheel-ruts. Chicory blossoms lined the way with their deep sky-blue that the eye can never quite reach the end of, echoed by the fainter tones of innumerable asters. Hoof-prints of deer were thick in the softer places. A partridge, with a startling explosion of wings, shot away through the thicket. A squirrel scolded the intruder in voluble falsetto. Cedar waxwings fluttered on before me and gathered again in sibilant twenties and thirties. Robins and bluebirds, lovers of the open spaces in earlier summer, were here in this upland covert in multitudes, doing nothing, for their year's work was over, but restless, flying with faint calls from bush to bough and back again, fluttering uncertainly, so that all the undergrowth seemed alive with the whir and beat of aimless wings.

After a mile of winding between the leaves, my road turned downhill, and its lyric beauty was changed at once into grandeur. It opened first into an avenue of leafless ash trees, rigid and gray in death, standing in strict formation all down the hill and up the farther slope like a double line of soldiers suddenly destroyed by some lethal gas but not yet fallen down. On one side ran a huge stone wall — five feet high, five feet thick, and a mile long — a work of gigantic toil. Little by little the road discovered a prospect of many-channeled hills to the west and north, rising tier above tier in graduated tones of blue and dimmer blue to the faint horizon. The sun was going down beyond this mysterious country, and the wind that blew from over the heights of Union was the voice of the wilderness. A fiery cloud blotted the sun for a moment, and all the land went suddenly gray. Then I topped the last domelike hill and saw the spire of Fairford church shining far away below me.

There is for some of us a keener thrill of adventure in entering a little town at twilight for the first time than in a first visit to an old and famous city. We know what to expect of London, Paris, Rome, for we have been living there, in a sense, many years; but a town like Fairford is all mystery. It may be the perfect town we have been looking for all our days. Hope revives at the first glimpse of its lighted windows, the heart quickens a little, and we go forward with our illusions carefully wrapped about us, prepared for the impossible.

The long pale finger of Fairford spire, rising slenderly among the trees, is all of the village that one can see at first as he goes down Ragged Hill into the valley of the Natchaug, and round about it the hills make a rich deep setting of verdure and rounded slopes. Then comes an outlying cottage or two, and at last, while the road still plunges down and down, there comes the glint of a stream running smoothly between little hills and among pastures graced by wine-glass elms.

To most of the towns in this neighborhood all the roads must climb, but Fairford lies snug in a twisting valley with the voice of water all about it. Those who know New England well do not need to be told much more about one of its little towns than that it stands on a hill or in a bottom, for either statement paints a picture. The motives that caused our ancestors to settle so frequently on the hilltops, where the soil was thin and the winds of winter bitterest, are not quite clear even to-day, after a good deal of clever theorizing; but at any rate we may say that whereas the hill towns began unconsciously to prepare, two centuries and more ago, for the summer residents of to-day, Fairford began by thinking of itself. Therefore the town is still practically undiscovered. There is no railroad near it, and although it is unfortunately bisected by an automobile highway, its few white houses make only a momentary blur on the landscape for those who hasten through. . . . I do my best to protect its privacy by giving it a fictitious name.

How long this isolation will continue no man can say, but we can be fairly sure that here, as elsewhere, 'commonness will prevail.' I always feel that I have reached the best places — of which I take Fairford, with all its faults, to be one — just in the nick of time, before they vanish away. It is a world, as some one has probably observed before, of imperfections and approximations, even in Connecticut. Fairford itself is not an ideal town; it only reminds one, vaguely, of the ideal. Otherwise, of course, I should have got no farther. For what is it that makes the rambler buckle on his pack in the early morning, take his stick from the corner, and strike out again on the road that has no end? Simply his dream, never fading because never entirely realized, of 'that flying Perfection round which the hands of man shall never close.'

I came into Fairford Center just before sunset, was hospitably received at the inn, and then, after telling my host what I would have for dinner, made my way at once to the central ganglion of all such towns as this, the front porch of the post-office and general store. Half a dozen leading citizens were already assembled there for the regular evening session, and with these I ingratiated myself, as much as it is possible for a man in knickerbockers to do with such a group on such short notice, by making humble inquiries about the weather probable for the morrow. These inquiries were referred to the local expert in meteorology, who opined *ex cathedra* that it would rain. (It did not.) The weather gambit led, as it always will when carefully handled, into a discussion of the season's crops, wherein I did not shine, and that in turn led into politics, in which again, for reasons of party affiliation of which I thought it best to say nothing, I gave no very brilliant account of myself. At last, with leisurely sweeps, the talk veered round to local gossip, which had been my goal throughout. What I wanted was to hear Fairford talking about itself. Just when it began to do so, I was summoned to supper.

Returning an hour later, I found the witenagemot still in session. The six men on the porch had not changed their positions, apparently, during my absence, and I was delighted to find that the place I had left was still vacant, as though they had expected me to return. (The probability is, however, that no one had felt any desire to move.) I opened this time by asking a gentle and sweet-voiced senior, whose white beard I could just see glimmering beside me in the darkness, about a farm-hand by the name of Sheppey with whom I had descended Ragged Hill that afternoon. 'He told me,' said I, 'that he was eighty-two, and yet he hadn't a white hair on his head. And he said that his wife is older still.'

The long white beard shook with tolerant laughter, and then the voice remarked, in the tone of a man who has made his peace with all human frailties: 'Sheppey always says he's eighty-two. He's been a-sayin' it for years and years. If he keeps on a-sayin' it long enough it'll come true some o' these times, I shouldn't be supprised. An' the way it seems to me is, he says it jest to make hisself seem more interestin' like, as you might say. But if you was to ask me, I don't guess that Sheppey is more than *sixty*-two years old, if he is a day. Why, I know'd that Sheppey when he first come to town. He come from Rhode Island, some town on the Bay . . . I don't just rec'lect the name of it at this present moment. Well, he was quite a young fellow then. Scarcely more'n a boy, as you might say. And yet it don't seem so very long ago to me, either, that he first come here. Eighty-two! Why, that's 'most as old as *I* be! I tell you he jest says that to make hisself more interestin' to strangers like yourself. . . . But his wife, she *is* old. Older than God, seemingly. Joe, how old'd you say Bill Sheppey's wife is now?'

Joe began at once upon an elaborate computation which involved many minute bits of evidence from local history, all of which I found entertaining. (Oh, the peace there is for a man with weary nerves and brain in sitting in the dark on the Fairford post-office porch discussing the ages of Bill Sheppey and his wife! My thoughts flashed back for an instant to the roar of Amsterdam Avenue, and then returned — how willingly! — to those drawling country voices.) This Joe, it appeared, was a brief abstract and chronicle of Fairford times, early and late. The grand total of years he worked out for Bill Sheppey's wife I do not now recall, but I assure the reader that he can hardly imagine her more venerable than she finally turned out to be. I judged that she might easily have been Bill's grandmother. But then, Fairford people are famous, among other things, for longevity. There was a woman then living in the town who confessed to one hundred and seven years, and who, furthermore, was said to be a real daughter of the American Revolution . . . not a daughter several times grand and great, but actually the daughter of a man who bore arms in the Continental Army. This seemed to me just possible, so that I thought it best not to investigate, but to accept the assertion on trust — observing meanwhile how the social value of this particular ancestry seems to increase directly with the remoteness of the descent.

My porch-mates gave me the main outlines of a quarrel that had been raging for some time between the Methodists and Congregationalists of the town and that was just then coming to a head. As I recall it, the members of the two denominations had agreed some months before to hold union meetings in their respective church buildings for six months at a time, turn and turn about, dividing the expenses. It was alleged that the Congregationalists had broken the agreement after the first few months and had gone back to their own church, taking their funds with them. The entire Methodist population of the town, twelve in number, was to hold a mass meeting on the next day but one to consider what they should do. The mass meeting promised to be a lively affair, and I was advised to arrange my engagements so that I might attend.

Nearly every man on the porch contributed his quota to the telling of this story, and each man spoke with a complete freedom from rancor and *odium theologicum* that left me wondering. For I knew that nearly every person in Fairford who had any religion worth mentioning must be either Congregational or Methodist, just as every adult must be either Democrat or Republican. I knew also that during the long years when religion was more important to Fairford than all other things together, such a question as this would have set the whole town — men, women, children, and dogs — by the ears. But not one of the men on the porch showed the slightest tinge of hatred for either of the contending parties; rather, they all seemed mildly amused at both of them. Perhaps they were on their good behavior, but if so they performed with remarkable unanimity and gave a very good imitation of brotherly love. A possible explanation, which I hesitate to mention, flashed through my mind — were they all of them godless free-thinkers?

In the group that gathers nightly at the Fairford post-office could be found, I think, the same mingling of ignorance and wisdom, heroism and futility, tragedy and humor and pathos, that Hawthorne discovered ninety years ago in the similar group at North Adams. Nothing essential has changed. And when proper allowances are made for the cramping effects of a narrow social environment, for lifelong toil, for remoteness from the main currents of modern life, these philosophers of the porch are far from contemptible. I sat with them for two hours, all the time in darkness, so that I had to judge them almost entirely by their voices and by what they said. Now and then some one would touch a match to his pipe, drawing the flame far down, and then a ruddy face would leap for five seconds out of the gloom — a face I had never seen before and shall not see again. In every instance it was somehow interesting, had some not quite obliterated mark of breeding, was worn by labor and, so it seemed to me, by thought. One or two of these men certainly did think. They seemed to live, indeed, for thinking, and for talk. It was as though they had generalized the determination of the Yankee not to be 'taken in' until it had become a mellow scepticism about all things celestial and mundane — and this, of course, is a mental attitude of dignity and charm. They seemed to me clearly superior in knowledge, skill, wisdom, and above all in personality, to the white-collar brigades of the city street. Each man stood out by himself, alone. In those two hours of talk on the dark porch I saw more human nature than

I had found during two months in New York City. . . .
But here, of course, I had it isolated, and I was looking
for it.

After some two hours among the Fairford senators I
crossed the road to my inn, and there I found that an
automobile party had just arrived and had taken rooms
for the night. These people lost no time, after I joined
them on the piazza, in giving me all the information
any one could have desired about themselves. It
seemed to be expected that I should reciprocate, but
I remembered Hazlitt's remark that 'the *incognito* of an
inn is one of its striking privileges,' and so chose like
him 'to baffle prejudice and disappoint conjecture.'
My statement that I was walking across Connecticut
cast a momentary chill upon the gathering, but they
soon continued the vivacious account of what they had
eaten and drunk, and what they had paid for it, during
the brief excursion into Maine from which they were
now returning.

A woman of middle age, who talked for all Fairford
to hear above the drone of falling water, was chief
spokesman for the group. 'We just now come down
from Glowster,' she shouted. ' *You* know . . . Glowster
on Cape Ann . . . little rocky burg with streets running
every which way. An' say, but we did see a lot o'
freaks up there! Same thing at Providencetown. They
was a-settin' out along the roads all day long, so's you
c'd hardly walk, and paintin' little pitchers of this an'
that. Maybe just a stone wall or only a tumble-down

old shack. And believe me, they didn't any o' them seem to have no fynancial support *at* all, and not likely to get any that way either.'

'No ma'am,' I replied in my suavest Philistine tones, 'it doesn't seem likely that they ever will while the public remains what it is to-day.'

'You *said* it,' she agreed with emphasis. 'And what I always say is, people's got to work if they want to have anything, and if they won't work, but only set around all day long in the sun paintin' little pitchers of this and that so's you can't hardly tell what it's a pitcher of when they get through, and then maybe try to sell it for as much as a hundred dollars and more, why, what I always say is they deserve all they get, or *don't* get.'

'Yes indeed,' I assented again. 'I know two or three of that kind myself who certainly deserve a good deal of what they don't get.'

This remark puzzled her for a moment, as though she detected in it a slightly alien note. Deciding, however, to give me the benefit of the doubt, she replied once more with her vigorous affirmative: 'You *said* it.'

Five minutes of this talk, which soon degenerated into a glowing account of her dining-room furniture at home — it had cost nine hundred dollars and was cheap at the price — was enough to remind me that walkers should be early to bed. As I went up the stairs I wondered, not for the first time, why it is that chance association with such persons should make me feel so uncomfortably foreign. With my friends of the post-office porch I had felt quite at home and had taken no little pride in the thought of our compatriotism. If they were not real Americans, where were any such to be found? Yet this woman, in five minutes, had made me feel a stranger in a strange land. It did not lessen my perplexity to remember that her language had shown certain inimitable but unmistakable reminiscences of the Yiddish tongue.

When I closed my book an hour later and looked out of the window, Fairford had dwindled into the faint ribbon of road below, the glimmer of a white housefront, and the music of many voices. It was a surprise to find how vocal so still a place could be. The quiet of the sleeping village was embroidered with delicate figures of sound that made it heard more clearly. Right across the dark fabric of that stillness the voice of the stream went wandering down, and I could distinguish the deep monotone of falling water at the dam from the treble voices of little waves under the bridge where they gathered from the plunge and loosened and began to run. Over the song of the stream, now rising and now falling but always joyous and triumphant, rang the multitudinous music of the crickets. It seemed to me while I was falling asleep that I had never before heard so many crickets, and that every leaf and grass-blade must hold a singer. My thoughts wandered away and were lost in a maze of tone, a wilderness of intricate syncopations. Two of these musicians at my window-sill were playing five notes against seven like the two hands of a consummate pianist, and a katydid crossed

their rhythms with the deeper tones of his tiny 'cello.
Just on the edge of sleep I heard the thrilling cry of the
hoot-owl on the wing — 'Hoo-hoo, hoo, hoo, hoo-hoo!'
Then all the voices blurred together and sank away.

MIRAGE

The Town Beyond the Mountain,
   Where we have never been,
Shines in a sunset glory
   Ineffably serene.

Above the small white houses
   Its lofty elm trees blow
A more mysterious music
   Than any trees we know.

Noon wears the color of eve there,
   And the song of its narrow stream
Comes down from a hidden country
   Deep in the hills of dream.

There Quietness keeps her dwelling
   And Peace descends like snow
On the Town Beyond the Mountain . . .
   Where we shall never go.

V

IN PRAISE OF LITTLE TOWNS

I love every stile and stump and lane in the village, and as long as I can hold a brush I shall never cease to paint them.
— JOHN CONSTABLE

 FAIRFORD, as I have said, is not an ideal town; it only reminds one, vaguely, of the ideal. Yet I think I may ask the reader to pause with me here while I try to describe the perfect town of which it reminded me and for which I was looking all along the Connecticut boundaries. I do this for two good reasons: because Connecticut was originally — and in several important respects is still — merely an assemblage of little towns, the State itself being an afterthought; and because the wholly justifiable satire that has recently been levelled against such dismal blots on the map as Spoon River and Gopher Prairie bids fair, unless we preserve some sharp distinctions, to distort our notion of one of the most beautiful things that men have made.

I remember how my traveling companion of years ago looked at Niagara Falls as one should look at an overgrown office building, and pronounced the opinion

that they were 'out of all proportion.' But when we came somewhat later to a nameless rivulet pouring  down between two hills, he bent lovingly beside the water where it slipped over a green stone and said: 'This is better than Niagara. I can get my arms around it.'

Beneath those offhand words I suspect there lies a whole philosophy of dolls and of idols, with the prolegomena of other matters more important still. They explain the almost universal passion for 'graven images' which only the Chosen People were not permitted to indulge, and also the pathetic waxen figures that we find snuggled to mummied bosoms — laid there four thousand years ago, in distrust of Isis and Osiris, to companion little Egyptian girls across eternity. They remind me that, although we may stand like gaping rustics wondering up for a time at things merely huge or abstract, we always go home with a sigh of content at last to the little and the concrete. And now that nearly everything about us is towering up into the gigantic and we find ourselves, with just the same old human needs, in a world apparently devised for titans, they help me to understand why it is that the wise among us are seeking ever more and more earnestly for a way out of Brobdingnag into some remnant of that earlier world in which man was still 'the measure of all things.' Sooner or later, they imply, we must accept our human limitations as final, even in the choice of waterfalls. We cannot embrace Niagara.

To the ancient Greeks this lowly humanism was instinctive. How boldly they drew down the gods, how tenderly they lifted Nature to their human level! Dwelling in a little land, they subdivided it into portions so small that the patriot could survey his entire country from a hilltop. His foot was always on his native heath. He was indigenous to that precise cranny of time and space in which he grew. . . . But we are mostly exotics at odds with our spatial or temporal climates — some of us belated Elizabethans or procrastinating Greeks knocking aimlessly about in the twentieth century, and others as far astray among the meridians as these among the years. They managed these things better when one had to start the machinery of the Holy Roman Empire in order to pass from the parish of one's birth to that adjoining. To-day we are sown by the wind, and a man may be born anywhere, without regard to his ancestral memories. The descendant of mountaineers is exiled to a prairie and the son of a sailor must content himself with a hillside brook.

Among so many diagnoses of *la maladie moderne*, one more may be safely ventured. Perhaps it is chiefly homesickness that ails us. And if so, what better object can a man propose for his more sentimental journeys than to find that special nook of the world for which he was really destined and designed? The belief that there is such a place dies hard in us — a place that would fit like an old shoe round our idiosyncrasies and would be tolerant of our most unreasonable whims, and one that we should know at the first glance as though we had lived there always. And, in fact, the world is full of weary nostalgic travelers, each of whom is in love with a place he has never seen. He does not know whether it is near or far, hemmed in by hills or bordered by the tides; he only knows that he will be sick for home until he finds it. Often he fears that it is only the ghost of some very ancient city long ago worn out of human remembrance, or else a mirage of the fancy like the lost Atlantis. But really the place he is seeking may be neither far away nor forgotten nor fabulous. It may be a little town.

If the little town is home, the poets should have told us; but there has been only one poet of the Golden Mean, and he died long ago. The others have been shouting alternate strophes and antistrophes to the city and the wilderness so long and loudly that they cannot summon strength for an epode. Without forgetting Goldsmith's Auburn or the

> Little town by river or seashore
> Or mountain-built with peaceful citadel

that was so strangely depopulated by a Grecian urn, one feels that the poets of England have done less than might have been expected, certainly far less than the painters, for this thing so intensely though not exclusively English. Yet they have known and loved it, as a thousand affectionate allusions show, and the English poets of our own day have celebrated their little towns as the Elizabethans did the ladies of their sonnets.

In prose the yield is somewhat better. William Cobbett knew more little towns, at least superficially, than any man before or since his time — knew them as a lover, mourned their decay, and gave the best years of his sturdy manhood to save them. Washington Irving is not easily surpassed as a connoisseur. Hazlitt loved a good inn as perhaps no other Englishman except Fielding has ever done, and the inn was still in his day the  stomach and brain at once of the little town. As for Stevenson, what was he but a eupeptic Scotch avatar of Hazlitt? Then there is Alexander Smith, whose 'Dreamthorpe' we could not well do without, and still other Scotchmen — John Galt, George MacDonald, and the creator of 'Thrums.' And of course it would never do to forget W. H. Hudson, probably the master of them all. In a letter that lies before me, written a year before his death, he says: 'But the subject of little towns is a long one — one for a very long conversation — one I should love to tire the sun with talking about.' He did talk about that subject through at least half a dozen volumes, and tired no one.

For reasons worth investigation, women have shown rather more native instinct than men for little towns, and our list would be poor indeed were it not for the names of Jane Austen, Miss Mitford, George Eliot, Mrs. Gaskell, Emily Dickinson, Mrs. Deland, and Mary E. Wilkins Freeman. On the fly-leaf of his 'Cranford' every amateur should write '*ne plus ultra*.' Yet there is an accidental classic of earlier date that might be advanced as a rival. Certainly the Reverend Gilbert White was more concerned about the hibernation of swallows than with spreading the fame of his native village, but we discern that he loves best the plants that grow in Selborne meadows and the birds that nest in the village elms. His love of place has won him thousands of readers who care nothing for his patience and accuracy. To one little plot of English ground he had a devotion exactly like the love of Thoreau for Concord.

Having named Thoreau, one has said nearly all, for he was not only the little town's philosopher and champion; he was its masterpiece. He said harsh things about Concord, and thought the townsfolk scarcely fit company for the autumnal maples, but yet he stayed there all his life, driving down year by year a deeper root and making the universe circle round his door. 'I think nothing is to be hoped from you,' he said, 'if this bit of mould beneath your feet is not sweeter to you than any other in this world, or in any world.' And again he writes to a friend: 'The old coat that I wear is Concord. It is my morning robe and study gown, my working dress and suit of ceremony. And it will be my nightgown at the last.' All that a wise man need know of trade he learned at the village fair; the hum of industry and commerce floated to him on the rumble of

the farmer's wagon; he saw in the silent rafts of boat-
men on the little Musketaquid all the fleets of merchant
navies round the world. Only a little town could have
made him what he was — acrid, angular, proud, and
full of the ancient wisdom of Mother Earth.

A true enthusiast would rather be silent than be misunderstood. Imagine the chagrin of a trout fisherman
who discovers, after holding forth
on the joys of angling, that his
hearers picture him sitting in the
blistering sun 'plugging' for horn-
pout! Just so the little town has
been confused with a very different
thing, a thing really ridiculous and
an ancient butt of ridicule. For
satire swings a slashing weapon — not a neat and dis-
criminating rapier but a broadsword or a battle-ax; and
lest the real culprit escape, it slaughters the innocent
bystanders. An unfortunate result of this is that the
mere mention of little towns rouses memories of parochial intolerance, Mother Grundyism, polysyllabic
country editors, and band concerts on Saturday afternoons. Under such circumstances, what can one say?
One maintains a compassionate silence.

But of course there are many differences between the
contentedly *little* town and the town that has the mis-
fortune to be merely small. These differences are not
so broad and glaring that he who rides may read, but
neither are they so subtle that he who walks need miss

them. Æsop's bullfrog became ridiculous only when, forgetting his batrachian limitations, he inflated his chest in the effort to resemble an ox. The small town is like that bullfrog. Determined to grow, and suffering already with illusions of grandeur, it lacks the dignity of modest content and so falls legitimate prey to ridicule. It is merely a stage in a process of becoming, with all the awkwardness of adolescence visibly upon it. Gazing steadily toward an alluring to-morrow, it ignores an obviously slipshod to-day and forgets whatever makeshift for a past it may have had. But the true little town basks serenely in the present, though with many a lingering look behind. It sets up no bill-board, either in fact or in effect, reading WATCH US GROW.

It should have a comfortable number of inhabitants, for 'a ship an inch long is not a ship,' as Aristotle pointed out, 'because it would be impossible to row it;' but there is a wavering upper limit beyond which the population cannot safely go. Ideally, each inhabitant should know all the others. The family trees of a genuine little town have spread and tangled into such a banyan thicket that each man speaks of his neighbor if not kindly at least cautiously, as of one who is probably a blood relation. Malicious gossip is found chiefly in the growing town that does not live on its own resources but is constantly appraising new human material from the outside world. . . . With these facts in mind, one might say, if pressed for figures, that a little town of two thousand persons is nearing the dead-line. If it expands beyond that limit, it is in danger of growing small.

But the blessedness of little towns does not consist wholly in their littleness. Other things are more important in their delicate fusion of amiable qualities, and among these nothing is more interesting than their way of dealing with time. There are some towns and cities that shed the centuries down from them as a mountain pine sheds its burden of snow, seeming cursed with an eternal youth, like gaunt stone walls that neither ivy nor moss will ever clothe; and there are others, less than half their age, that lie already heavily encrusted with years. These are the true children of Time. The earth seems older because of them, and one would say that the hills had been heaped up about them as an afterthought. All genuine little towns are very old. An appreciable interval is usually necessary for the growth of a small town into a large one, but it takes far longer to make any town properly little. It must be seasoned by many winters and ripened by many a summer sun. As in the aging of wine or the coloring of meerschaum, time is of the very essence of the problem. It is perhaps more necessary than even a river.

Nothing shows more clearly than little towns, however, how slightly our sense of the antique is dependent upon calendars and almanacs. Chronology can tell us almost nothing about the real age of a town, for the question is only whether its thought of itself is forward- or backward-looking. To the imagination of Nathaniel Hawthorne Salem was more aged than Rome, and he sated his enormous passion for antiquity in the Old Manse at Concord, a house barely seventy years old when he went there. One would suppose from the account he gives of the house in the 'Mosses' and elsewhere that it must have been more like seven hundred. Just as we are told that there are some savages who can count only by their twenty toes and fingers, and that they are reduced, when these have been outnumbered, to a vague and awe-stricken 'many,' so it appears that the largest unit of time we can really manage imaginatively is that provided by the longest human life. When a town lays down that yardstick more than once, when it gets beyond the depth of the oldest inhabitant, then it has achieved longevity enough and is already 'one with Nineveh and Tyre.' In his *oraison funèbre* on Cambridge, the little town that died when he was young, James Russell Lowell made this clear. 'As well rest upon the first step,' said he, 'since the effect of what is old upon the mind is single and positive, not cumulative. As soon as a thing is past, it is as infinitely far away from us as if it had happened millions of years ago.' According to this sound doctrine, the little towns of America cede nothing in the matter of age to those of the Old World. We have many a gray town 'where men grow old and sleep under moss-grown monuments.' Some of them have been ancient for centuries.

Like most things that are old, the little town has a strong instinct for self-preservation. Curiosity does not surprise its secrets, condescending patronage is quietly rebuked, well-intentioned reformers are crumpled against the stone walls of its conservatism. It perpetuates itself by an untiring resistance of change and by refusing to advertise. Well knowing that if its tiny taper were set upon a hill it would inevitably go out, the little town takes no shame in hiding its light under a bushel. A river it should have, as a silver link with the outer world, else it lives in an isolation too complete, and is not merely remote but separate. This river, however, should serve chiefly spiritual ends, and should be navigable by nothing much more mercantile than a canoe. Furthermore, the town should be inaccessible by rail and the roads should not be such as to encourage approach by automobile. All this follows as a matter of course from the little town's motto: '*Odi profanum vulgus et arceo.*'

One cannot be too emphatic about the necessity of bad roads, for they are the town's defensive rampart and home-guard, without which it goes very rapidly the melancholy way that nearly all good trout streams have gone, and for the same reason. It is chiefly because the roads have been not quite bad enough that the present eulogy so narrowly misses being an elegy. The direst foe of the little town is not storm or fire or flood, but gasoline; it can weather the centuries bravely and its old age is heartier than its youth, but it suddenly crumbles and falls, like Jericho, at the sound of the horn.

'God made the country and man made the town,' but to make a little town requires the coöperation of both. No other thing is so natural and yet so human. It clings as close to earth as a lichen to a weathered stone, yet it is not wild. With his customary precision, Mr. Thomas Hardy has made this clear in his descrip-tion of Casterbridge: 'Bees and butterflies in the cornfields at the top of the town, who desired to get to the meads at the bottom, took no circuitous course, but flew straight down High Street without any apparent consciousness that they were traversing strange latitudes. And in autumn airy spheres of thistledown floated into the same street, lodged upon the shop fronts, blew into drains; and innumerable tawny and yellow leaves skimmed along the pavement, and stole through people's doorways into their passages, with a hesitating scratch on the floor, like the skirts of timid visitors.'

Besides its merely natural beauty drawn from the dust and dew, the little town wears a look of homely pathos that has grown upon it through many years of human joy and grief. The hands are dust that planted its lofty trees; its doorsills are hollow from the tread of feet that stepped long ago over another threshold. In some ways it may seem more human than those that built it or those that now go up and down the streets. It is like the wood of an old violin that has sounded and throbbed so long with passions not its own as to have forgotten the sunny and wind-swept forest where it grew.

Where else do men and women live on more friendly

terms with all that surrounds them than in these tiny
islets of humanity? Both sides have given too many hos-
tages — men to the churchyard mould and Nature to

barn and croft — for them to keep up the ancient feud;
the boundary lines are so faded and forgotten that one
can no longer be sure what is human there and what is
not. It is no idle fancy that sees in the townsfolk mere
conscious and concentrated glebe and tillage, just as
the grass of God's Acre is only green and blowing man.
In a little town of southern New Hampshire lie the

bones of one William Cambridge, laid there early in
the eighteenth century. A pine tree three feet through
the trunk has grown about the headstone, snapping it
in two and lifting the part bearing the man's name
away from the lower portion. How much of the pine
is now William Cambridge and how much of William
Cambridge is now coniferous, it would take the genius
of a Sir Thomas Browne to compute; but certainly
there is enough of the man in the tree to warrant its
use of his name. William Cambridge now waves his
lofty green-blue needles in the breeze, he nods to
Wachusett and beckons to Monadnock, and the birds
build their nests in his branches. His great-grand-
children may some day cut him down and build themselves a house out of their ancestor.

The supreme test of the little town is its human product. By a delicate mingling of freedom with restraint,
publicity with privacy, multitude with solitude, and
above all by patient collaboration with time, it shapes
a kind of character not easily found elsewhere; and the
mark of that character is reasonableness, fidelity to
fact, unswerving belief in moral cause and effect. In
the great city, what with the law's delay and our skill
in keeping up appearances, what with our substitution
of mere counters for the things they represent, only
those of alert imagination keep their grip upon fundamental realities. Not so in the little town. Comfort on
a winter's night is closely associated in the minds of its
people with the thought of wood once standing in a

definite wood-lot, and then cut and hauled and split; the thought of stocks and bonds, of landlords and janitors, or of coal strikes, does not enter in. Surely this nearness of the concrete, this immediate and calculable response of Nature to effort put forth, must have a tonic moral effect. Charity is not impeded there by any uncertainty as to who is one's neighbor. Social criticism of folly and wickedness is immediate, inevitable, direct. In such a place, if anywhere, one may see life steadily and see it whole; and there is a wisdom in those who have grown old there which is unlike the wisdom found in cities or in books, and which they owe to their privilege of studying steadily and at close range full-length living examples of wisdom and folly, virtue and vice.

A few of the wisest men have seen that one needs for the 'proper study of mankind' a place where acquaintance may deepen year by year into love and where character is given time to open out before one's eyes. After many years of eager life in the great city, Montaigne went back to the little town of his childhood, and there his knowledge ripened slowly, as on a southern wall, into the mellow wisdom of the Essays. He it was who reversed the famous sentence of Julius Cæsar, saying that he would rather be the second or third man in his native village than the first man in Paris. But there is a still more familiar instance. Biographers have exhausted absurdity in trying to explain why Shakespeare returned to Stratford, giving up, at the height of his fame and powers, the moving spectacle of London, the seething cosmopolis of the Bridge, and the little world of Paul's Walk — turning his back on the plaudits of the Bankside, Blackfriars, and the Court to gossip over fence-rails about pigs and geese with the yokels of Warwickshire. But no one who understands little towns makes a wonder of this. In reality, nothing in Shakespeare's London life became him like the leaving of it. That final gesture of farewell is almost worth the masterpieces he might have remained to write. London had taught him tricks of the trade, but Stratford had made him a poet. Knowledge had come in such measure that he felt all the more need of the wisdom that still lingered. He had looked too deeply into human hearts to be content any longer with partial glimpses; he had lived too deeply to endure any longer a hurried and distracted life. . . . Or so, at any rate, the lover of little towns makes it out. 'What do you do here in your lonely mountain hamlet?' a supercilious traveler is said to have asked a native of Vermont. The answer came back edged with an irony that may not have been fully intended or wholly understood: 'Oh, we just live.' Shakespeare may have been as wise as that.

Quite naturally and simply, his day's work ended and his wages taken, he went home to his little town. And even in death he clung to it, if we may trust the strange minatory epitaph. Did he guess that the arrogant city that could not hold him living would certainly claim him dead, and try to erase the shame of his Stratford birth by a splendid metropolitan inter-

ment? Did he remember the seven cities that con-
tended for Homer? — proving thereby that Homer belonged to no city. However this may be, every friend
of little towns should rejoice that for three hundred
years a sufficient watch and ward has been kept above
him by those final caustic words: Curst be he that
moves my bones.'

If only for the reason that little towns are composed
of human beings, some imperfections are to be expected.   Indeed, not the least
delightful of them often seem
miraculously fortunate combina-
tions of faults and flaws — but
only their lovers should speak of
this and only lovers should hear.
Their shortcomings merely remind us again that human nature is very prevalent.   Although
they have their due proportion of vicious, weak, and
foolish persons, the influence of the wise and sober is
more effective in them than elsewhere. It has been
said that 'if Sodom had been a little town, its few
righteous would have been enough.'

Our country supports the little town with the amused
tolerance that an oyster may be imagined as feeling
toward its pearl. Being the product of generations of
careful selection, having withstood for many years the
strong winnowing of commercialism, it has of course
a strange look to us. The city gathers by blind chance

its random millions, but the little town selects its tens
and dozens by a seduction all its own. If it has the look
of an exotic among us, that is because it has been here
so long. Nearly all that America stands for is im-
plicit in its government, ideals, and daily routine. Our
little towns are the very seed from which we sprang,
and despite the insolence of metropolitan parvenus,
which are after all only their giant brood, they still
present the typical and also the most favorable aspect
of American life. I hope and think that they may yet
see the great cities all to bed.

Although much of what is said against little towns
is due to ignorance, some of it should be attributed
to the familiarity that breeds contempt. The wise

amateur avoids both extremes,
choosing for his example not
George Crabbe but Oliver Goldsmith, who knew most of the
villages of Europe but lived in
London. The amateur knows
that some things are best seen,
not only most favorably but
most truly, through a haze of distance; he doubts
whether those who live in little towns know them
best. They may have acquired them by a meritless
inheritance, and so may never have known the joys of
search, discovery, and recognition. As for himself, he
would no more live in one than Dante would have
set up housekeeping with Beatrice, or Sir Galahad

have drunk his evening beer from the Holy Grail. He
is aware that the ideal little town, as I have tried to
describe it, may exist nowhere in substantial brick
and stone; but this does not greatly disturb him. To
any profane skeptic he might paraphrase the reply of
Socrates to Glaucon, who objected that he had never
seen or heard of such a place as the ideal Republic:
'How would a painter be the worse painter if it could
be shown, after he had painted a picture of an ideally
beautiful little town, that no such town existed? In
heaven, at least, there is laid up a pattern of such a
town.'

The amateur, I say, asserts a higher wisdom that
shuns impertinent knowledge. He observes a delicate
ritual of approach and departure, entering the little
towns of his pilgrimage at dusk and resolutely leaving
them in the early morning . . . . All a long September
day he has been moving down a valley road, with the
ripple of some companionable river never far away.
Town after town is strung like a bead on the silver
thread of his road, but he leaves them all reluctantly
behind. At evening he sees some final church spire
gleam against darkening fields in the last rays of the
sun, and he comes to it just as the lights begin to glow
in cottage windows, so that what he sees is less than
what he imagines as the charm of the place. And all
night long the mystery and strangeness of that little
town will be about him as he lies in his inn, hearing
at intervals, over the rushing voice of the river, the
steeple clock drone through the darkness. In the morn-

ing he will arise early and go on his way, so that before the dawn has faded out of the east he will be looking back from some distant height. And when he turns away for the last time he will know that nothing can ever tarnish or dim that picture painted on the walls of his dream — spire and river and hill shining there forever in the sunrise.

I SHALL REMEMBER

As I went down across the hills
   From Colne to Quenington
I saw the roofs of Bibury
   Shining in the sun.
I shall remember Bibury now
   Until my days are done.

I shall remember cottages
   Carved out of silver and gold,
And how the great beech-darkened hills
   Tenderly enfold
That little human island
   Washed round by meadow and wold.

And I shall think what life might be —
   Ah! if I had my will —
In some gray cottage crowned with thatch
   Down by the crumbling mill,
With the dull thunder of the weir
   Day-long beneath my sill.

When men shall tell me of the fields
   And hills and homes they love,
Bibury is the little town
   I shall be thinking of . . .
The arrowy stream, the winding road.
   And the gloom of the hills above.

One crooked street of weathered stone
  Is what I shall recall:
How slowly across the afternoon
  Its purple shadows crawl,
And how the reddening ivy-leaf
  Clings to the sun-washed wall.

Each man must have some memory
  Shining, as he grows old,
To light him through the stealing dark
  And keep his thoughts from cold.
I shall remember Bibury —
  Bibury-in-the-Wold.

VI

A NUMBER OF THINGS

Non ulla Musis pagina gratior
Quam quæ severis ludicra jungere
Novit, fatigatumque nugis
Utilibus recreare mentem.
— Dr. Samuel Johnson

 ALL that gives little Fairford the slightest place in the work-a-day world is its manufacture of various small articles of wood. The rapid stream is taken prisoner just above the town, is parceled into several narrow strips of silver, gathered again into a pool above a dam, and so made to turn a dozen wheels before it goes free at last below the bridge with a shout of deliverance. All about the town one hears, over the voice of running water, an intermittent scream of saws, and the place is pervaded by magical odors of new-cut and of rotting wood, of bark and tannin and turpentine.

I knew, therefore, when I set out on the north road towards Union that I should travel a thickly timbered region. From Fairford itself you can see the outposts of the forest entrenched along the hills, overlooking the small encampment of humanity that dwindles year by year, spying out the land, winning back a house-place here and an acre of arable there, reaching down a little farther every season.   You foresee the outcome: the forest is coming back. In Union it has never been dispossessed, and it has gathered itself together there and mewed its strength and bided its time until the invaders should be depleted or relax their vigilance. Five hundred years from now . . . well, one hesitates to say; but if the present tendency continues Fairford will then be merely a dot and a name on the maps of antiquarians. Any one of many chances may save it for five centuries, for five millennia, but the ultimate issue is not in doubt. The forest can afford to wait.

This refluent tide of the wilderness was all that I could think about as I went up the Union road under the pines, for I knew that what I saw going on at Fairford was typical of what I should find elsewhere in Connecticut, and symbolic of greater things. What had seemed in the valley an amicable partnership between man and nature took on here the aspect of combat to the death. Everywhere I went in the days that followed I saw one stage or another of man's ever-lasting struggle with the wild, and nearly everywhere I saw the marks of his defeat. In the country I walked across there are thousands of miles of stone wall running through unbroken woodland; I saw, without looking for them, at least two score of cellar-holes with large trees growing in them and dense thicket all about; I found orchards of centenarian apple trees engulfed by the forest. A farmer tried to show me from a hill-

top where his neighbors of thirty years ago had lived, asserting that he could then see a dozen houses from that very spot; but there was no house in sight from where we stood and the cleared fields of his youth were now a bosky 'stump-land' browsed by the deer.

To a thoughtful traveler these 'backward' parts of New England suggest and symbolize much more than they are, for in their three centuries they have traversed the main phases of civilization's rise, culmination, and decay. Scarcely any land that is so young in years now seems so old. Men began to hack and hew at this wilderness only yesterday, as our human past is measured, and their swift taming of it shows as clearly as anything what manner of men they were. Their culture took root at once in the congenially stubborn soil, produced its 'bleak blossom of scentless breath,' and then withered on the stem. And the pathos of this is not so much in the passing of old New England as in the sense, induced at times almost overpoweringly by her dying farms and villages, that all our noblest effort is doomed to futility. So many times we have dreamed great dreams and wrought heroically to bring them to pass. The fruition has often been fairer than that the Puritans attained, and often it has lasted longer in years, but the end has been the same. Think of Atlantis, hidden somewhere under the wandering waves, and the tree-strangled cities of Yucatan!

New England is a persuasive symbol not only of the wasted toil and hope of our long past but also of the wasted hope and toil that shall be. Connecticut alone,

and even little Fairford, suggests what may be the
nature of our end. We may go out, of course, in some
vast collision on the highway of the stars, some
splendid coda of fire and uproar consistent with our
estimate of the planet's importance; but this consummation, although devoutly to be wished, is too unlikely to hope for. The probability is that we shall
merely cool and dwindle. The final scene will scarcely
be that brilliant consummation of all we have done
and known that the cheerful apostles of automatic
progress imagine; for already we see that every gain is
bought by loss and that man's will is not able to hold
the heights it has the strength to win. Rather, I think,
it will be a scene of people old and cold and disillu-
sioned, far inferior in mental acumen to the men of
Greece, in wisdom to the seers of India, in sanity to
the sages of China, in energy and knowledge to ourselves. Year by year the forest will crowd back upon
us, blotting the fields we have cleared, blocking our
roads, erasing our boundaries and our 'No Trespass-
ing' signs, making merry havoc with all the little lines
and dots and printed names we have put down on the
map. London and Paris, Chicago and Manhattan
Island, even the Eternal City herself, will go as Fairford is now visibly going, until the oak and beech and
pine have taken back their own.

It may seem that these thoughts must have been out
of tune with the morning as I went along under the
trees on the road that climbs to Union, but I did not

find them so. A man who has made some temporary truce with himself over the thought of his own death and — what is more difficult — the death of all that is dear to him, can take a detached view of the planet's dissolution, for the part is greater than the whole. Indeed, there are some moods in which the slow cooling of the cinder on which we sprawl and spawn seems a beneficent catharsis, moods in which only lifeless things seem fit to endure. We feel this most keenly under the winter stars, when they are burnished by the north wind and pulsate with a chill perfection. Looking up through the clean air, we take pleasure in the thought that there may not be one body in all those multitudes that has suffered the accident we call life, and that if any have suffered it anywhere they are not among those we see but are dark stars, rather, gradually rotting away like our own. For the most part, hopelessly anthropocentric as we are, we think of the aging of our planet, because it has made us possible, as a growth toward maturity. A more detached intelligence would see that life never attacks a planet in its youth or prime but only when senile decay has cooled its vital heat, gouged wrinkles in its cheeks, and filled its eyes with rheum, making it ready for the sidereal bone-pile.

A mile or two beyond North Ashford I came to a tiny schoolhouse embowered by birch trees. Asters and goldenrod were blowing in the playground, and the drone of children's voices reading in unison came slumbrously through the open door. A hum of bees, like an echo of that murmur, filled the air with drowsy monotone. The sunshine lay more still and golden here than in the lanes behind me. Spilling from a profound sky, it fell among the chattering birch leaves and was broken into cascades of metallic glitter that gathered again among the grass-roots and slept in a broad pool, soaking slowly into the sod. Here, it seemed to me, a man might almost drown himself in sunshine. I decided to try it. Finding a strip of grass over the path from the school ground, I leant my back against the stone wall and drew forth my luncheon. When this was eaten I found a plentiful dessert of wild grapes hanging in heavy clusters a few feet away.

As I lay there, in the large content of a man who has gathered some part of his own dinner, a huge old farm horse came stumbling down the lane, scattering pebbles before the ponderous tread of his hooves, browsing here and there among the wayside herbage, and blowing mightily from time to time to clear the dust and pollen from his nostrils. He too was living off the country.

Without a strap of harness on him, or any other badge of servitude, he looked a perfect symbol of leisure honestly earned. It did me good to gaze at him. The beauty of a nervous thoroughbred is one thing, but the grandeur of his majestic muscles, enormous fetlocks, and mighty mane seemed to me better still because it answered to something deeper in my own mood. He was an epic horse, fit for Odin's riding. He made me understand better than before what the physician meant in telling the overworked and worried Ernest Pontifex to go out' to the Zoo and look at the large, grave animals. Small animals, he said, would not do at all, and he advised particularly against monkeys as being too much like the human race.

Solomon was probably right in urging the sluggard to go to the ant, but a tired man should consider a large and lumbering cart-horse on holiday. There is nothing more therapeutic. Of course I admit that much may be said for cows, but most of it has already been said by Walt Whitman and others. A cow, moreover, can scarcely be said to have any leisure because she never has anything else. Her tranquillity is superb, it is consummate; but then it is also professional. My farm horse was an amateur, enjoying his holiday all the more because it was not to be everlasting. I was hoping at every minute that he would lie down on his back and kick his heels in the air, but probably the lane was too narrow for this supreme exhibition of equine contentment, or else the ground was too rocky. I knew that he had it in him, for there were burrs on his back.

He shambled past me without so much as a glance in my direction, planting his huge hoof within six inches of my outstretched foot. I watched him down the hill until he was hidden by the flicker of sun and shade, and sent my blessing after him. More than any other creature that I met in all my journey he seemed bent upon some goalless errand like my own, as though he too had set aside a space of time out of his respectable, strenuous, and law-abiding year in which to drift across the Connecticut landscape thinking idle and self-pleasing thoughts in whatever order they might come. Of course I said to myself that he had the right idea. I thought that he could give lessons in the almost forgotten art of leisure to ninety-nine vacationists in the hundred — to all the fretful human midges that buzz from one excitement to another, that must be always making a noise, always entertained. . . . But then I remembered that only a creature of his ponderous strength could rest so mightily as he. A muscle, I said, is tested by its power of relaxation as much as by its tension, and a man also. If you want to know how a man can work, I said, see how he rests.

And then, as though to make myself the most brilliant possible example of high-power efficiency — for the benefit, perhaps, of the children when they came out of school — I made a pillow of my knapsack, pulled my cap over my eyes, and lay down among the asters with the sunshine splashing all about me. No thought of the indefinite miles that lay between me and any probable bed for the night disturbed my quiet. The busy hum of scholars across the lane and that of bees in the aster-bloom, so far from being a rebuke, was an incentive to slumber. Thoughts of the old farm horse rambling down the lane so full of sleep were a further soporific. I was surprised, not for the first time, to discover how staunchly the planet bears one up when it is allowed to do all the work. Usually, when we overdriven mortals lie down to sleep, we hold some muscle tense, some nerve drawn taut, as though our beds could not quite sustain us; strenuous even in sleep, we feel that we must struggle still against something, even though it be only the force of gravity. But there were eight thousand miles of earth in my mattress and I had put the strenuous life behind me by the width of several townships. The contrast between this nameless lane and Amsterdam Avenue was complete. I slept.

When I sat up at last among the asters and looked about me, the length of the eastering shadows was a warning that, even as a rambler, I must be on my way. A quarter of a mile brought me to a patriarchal farmhouse with wide verandas under elm trees and — what was more to the purpose — a well. While I stood drinking the water I had drawn, the cold pure sap of those granite hills, the farmer came out to talk with me. He looked as old as his house or the trees before it, but his eyes were frosty-clear under the gray sheds of his brows. He told me that he and his 'old woman' had lived here alone for many years, ever since the last of their children went off to the city. When I suggested that it might be lonely for them there, two very old people on the edge of a forest, he looked mildly indignant and said he had never found it so. But I had so often tried to imagine the lives of aged men and women in these desolate farmsteads that I pursued my question, perhaps a little ungently, asking him how he found it in the dead of winter when the roads were blocked, no mails came through, and he saw no one for weeks together. He answered that there were always the chores to do, and that in winter, when the days were short, it was nearly time to go to bed when the work was over.

It was a simple answer, and in its quiet way rather heroic. I was thrilled even while he spoke by the broad parabolic value of his words, for something like this, I realized, is what we all may say. The courage of human hearts, although I should want to be the last to disparage it, is not, after all, miraculous. This is how we manage to forget the solitude and the waiting shadow: we have our chores to do — or if there be any who have none, God help them! — and when our work is over it is nearly time to go to bed.

Facing the basic and elemental, we find parables on every hand. While the old man talked about his eighty years on this lonely farm, I hardly knew whether it was the voice of one man only to which I was listening or that of all mankind. He said that he had always lived here, with a suggestion that it would be absurd to feel lonely in the house of one's birth. Yes, no doubt. But as I looked out northward over the hills whence his winter winds would come and realized that there would be no lighted window except his own to illumine all those miles on a winter evening, his courage touched my heart.

Perhaps it is only the softened temper of the city that makes a wonder of such things, and certainly it was not for me, with some dregs of my youth still in me, to understand what a man of his years might find there to make him love his life. I saw that he had the strength of his native hills, not to be broken or turned aside. He was the kind of man that laid the stone walls of New England. There was something tonic in the mere sight of him, and I was glad to find that life could be worth living even on such harsh terms. Much would depend, of course, upon his 'old woman,' whom I did not see. I hoped that he would have her with him to the end, and that she might have him; but this, I knew, was unlikely. Another year, and he might be facing the winter quite alone. As I went down the road, trying to picture the farm on a January night, these verses gradually shaped themselves:

LANTERN LIGHT

Far up against the sunset walls
One gaunt and rigid oak tree sprawls,
Misshapen, weather-beaten, carved
In ebony, and reaches starved
Old frozen fingers up to hold
The last dim shred of dwindling gold.

Deep in the barn a lantern lights
An old man as he puts to rights,
Showing the glint of milking-pails,
Bright harness buckles, swinging tails,
Brown fetlocks buried deep in straw,
And, in the loft's capacious maw,
Huge tods of hay, like unkempt hair,
Pulled loose and hanging in the air.
It finds the blade of an old ax
Far in a corner, gleams through cracks,
And makes the cobweb at its side
A thing of wonderment and pride.

An hour behind the set of sun
The farmer's daily task is done.
He lifts the light down from the peg
And takes it with him. Leg and leg,
Lit by the swinging lantern, throw
Enormous shadows on the snow.
His crunching footfalls echo back
From the barn-door and dim haystack.

One failing lantern will not light
Ten square miles of a winter's night,
Nor can a man's own footsteps wake
More than the ghostly sound they make.
Shadow and echo and keen cold
Are all he has now. He is old.

But though the lantern, burning dim,
Shakes in the trembling hand of him,
Yet all the night is made aware
Of something dauntless moving there
That holds it steadily at bay. . . .
The shadows cower, and give him way.

He gains the porch, looks round once more,
And stoutly slams the farmhouse door.
And now, unless a shingle snaps
With frost, or an icy finger taps
Against his window, silence falls.
Cattle are quiet in the stalls.
The crow, perched in the frozen oak,
Ruffles his feathers for a cloak.

Then, after the last light of day,
Sifting from very far away,
Without a breath, without a sound,
Without a footfall on the ground,
Mysteriously comes the slow
Soft benediction of the snow.

Here began the forest of Union, one of the smallest
towns in the State and probably the wildest. This
forest is extensive enough to have made a respectable
king's hunt in the days when such things still existed,
and it is romantic enough for any taste, full of hills and
swamps, an admirable country for moose. I was glad
to learn that the Canadian lynx is sometimes met with
there, and I should not be surprised to hear that the
township supports a few bears. The approach to the
village is very beautiful, but as I have sworn not to
bore my reader with descriptions of landscape I shall

only say that four miles of up and down under hemlock boughs brought me to a barn on the very top of Union Hill. Inside the door of this barn were two men, seated on the floor, their backs resting against two sacks of feed. Because I had still ten or twelve miles to go and the afternoon was wearing rapidly away, I found this picture of almost Theocritean peace quite irresistible, and so I walked into the barn, got a third sack of feed for my own back, and sat down on the floor beside them in the sunshine.

I found it worth the cost in time to learn how serenely life goes by on Union Hill and what men talk about up there on sunny afternoons. Looking out from our great cave of shadow across the sun-swept miles, we talked first about land values, and I was told that the stump-land didn't 'vally at all,' but could be had almost for the asking. Then we came to local gossip, in which department one of my companions showed great erudition. Each of his stories was embellished by genealogical data in the generous rural fashion. His talk, strongly flavored by a broad Rabelaisian humor and vocabulary, was constantly running up family trees, which seemed to stand in Union about as thick as the pines in the forest.

What I liked most about these two men was their
power of resting. There is more labor of a hard grub-
bing sort to be done in Union than in almost any other
Connecticut township, and they had chosen a com-
manding position on the very top of the hill and looked
down upon all that work with profound serenity. The
very sight of it seemed to compose and soothe them.
For this reason, although I did not find them very wise
in other respects, I remember them as the philosophers
of the barn floor.

When I had sat for half an hour with these men of
leisure, I saw that the shadows were growing very long,
and so I said, reluctantly, that I must be on my way to
Stafford Springs and that I should be grateful for directions. There were the usual exclamations of amaze-
ment when they learned that I intended to walk all the
way, 'better'n ten mile,' but at length, finding that
there was no turning me from my folly, they constructed a map of the region by laying straws on the
floor, showing just what turns to take, and ending with
the inevitable words, 'You can't miss it.'

I had heard that phrase so many times, my powers
of losing my way had been so often grossly underestimated, that I was not reassured. And no sooner
had I reached the foot of Union Hill than I made some
crucial blunder that led me into a maze of wood-roads,
by-paths, cow-tracks, and rabbit-runs from which I
saw no escape unless by the light of another day. For
mile after mile I came to no occupied house. The
country was populated by nothing but ghosts, and

even these gave only furtive hints of their presence. Thus, with only the setting sun for guide, I stumbled on through thickets of thorn, under barbed-wire, over shad-fences, round boulders tree-top high, until I came to a tottering guide-post all green and gray with age. It may have been merely the specter of a guide-post standing there in that uncertain light, but it seemed to indicate, with a northward-pointing finger, that I was three miles from Wales and five from Holland. Surprised to find that I had wandered quite so far, I admitted that these twain were excellent countries and contained much admirable walking, but I declined the invitation on the ground that I was taking a journey in Connecticut. . . . I had blundered over the boundary line into Massachusetts.

THE READER — It seems to me, if I may be allowed to edge in a word, that this part of your book is somewhat less exciting than some other parts.

THE WRITER — Perhaps you might even like to suggest that this part of my book is positively dull.

READER — Well, seeing that you provide the word . . .

WRITER — Just so. There's nothing to be gained between you and me by circumlocution. And now that you have at last made yourself heard, pray continue.

READER — I hope you don't think that my interruption was discourteous.

WRITER — Oh, not in the least! It was only a little unconventional. I shall be glad to hear your excellent opinions at any time, for you can hardly imagine how lonely a writer gets to feel in the dead waste and middle of a book like this, and how cheering it is, therefore, to discover that one reader, at least, is still sticking doggedly to him. And besides, I hate a book that is one long monologue. The habit of writing such books puts a man too much on a level with clergymen and college professors, who never receive any frank criticism spoken courageously to their faces and so get to be — well, what we see. I am particularly grateful for your excellent remarks because they give me an opening for something I have felt, for a good many pages back, ought to be said on the general topic of tediousness.

READER — Don't you think that the practical illustrations you have already given of that matter might suffice?

WRITER — No, I should like to write a whole book about it. (At present I am not attempting to do so.) I should divide tedium into its various categories, classes, orders, genera, species, sub-species, and varieties, devoting a first chapter to the plain and easily tolerable tedium of dullards, whom God must love because he has made so many of them, and proceeding to the still endurable but more elaborate tedium of pedants and pedagogues and bookworms, going on from there to the pious tedium of professional moralists, to the terrible tedium of reformers and 'social servants' and uplifters, to the bigoted tedium of hard-headed business men, to the all but intolerable tedium of 'red-blooded' people, to the ineffable tedium of

'hundred-percenters' and patrioteers, and so on, in a
steadily upward sweep, until I came at the end to the
ultimate, the exquisite, the absolute tedium of those
who think there should be no tedium anywhere in life,
or even in books, and who would drive it away, extrude,
expel, extravasate, deracinate, averruncate, and send
it to Jericho by any means fair or foul — even by playing bridge-whist.

READER — But . . .

WRITER — If you will excuse me! Your helpful remarks had particular reference to the tedium of this
present book, or rather to that of some recent passages
in it. Now if you will be so good as to turn back to that
paragraph in which you found that you could contain
yourself no longer, you will find that I was there trying
to suggest how it feels to a weary man to be lost in the
brambly wilderness of Union with the night coming on,
no inhabited house anywhere about, and something
between ten and twenty miles yet to go before he can
hope to find a bed. I made that paragraph as short as
I could, leaving out a good many tedious things that
might well have been put into it if I had been determined to make quite clear how long and tedious that
hour of bush-whacking was to me.

READER — But . . .

WRITER — You were about to say that I should
have done well to skip the account entirely, or else to
enliven it with one of those digressions that have embellished earlier pages. As for skipping, am I to understand that you do not care to go along with me, taking

the dreary with the vivid miles, the shadow with the shine? Because if you do not, then 'out upon this half-faced fellowship'! And as for working in a digression, doubtless it could have been done; but I have tried to set down chiefly the thoughts that occurred to me at the time and in the place concerned. Beating about there in the brush at the foot of Union Hill, I did not think at all — unless about the rent in my coat, how long I should be able to sustain life on the few raisins left in my pocket, or whether I could light a fire to sit by during the night with my two matches. To expand such faint glimmers of idea as flit across a hungry and weary man's brain at the end of a long day in the open would be tedious indeed.

READER — But . . .

WRITER — And then there is another consideration that must be kept in mind, not only here but throughout this book. William Hazlitt inquires elaborately, you remember, at the beginning of his essay, 'On Going a Journey,' whether it is best to walk with a companion or alone. Wisely or not, I chose to take the journey here recorded without company. Had it been otherwise, I should be able in the duller parts of my story to depend upon the witty or profound remarks my companion would have made, but as things stand I must draw the matter of my digressions — which I am glad to hear you commend with such enthusiasm — solely from the conversations that went on, so to speak, between the two lobes of my own brain. The proper allowances should certainly be made.

Half a mile down the lane from that spectral guide-post I came to a tramp who was preparing his supper.

He had got him some five ears of hard corn out of a field as he came along, and these he was trying to boil in a black and battered little tin pail over a tiny fire of sticks. His fire did not prosper, and he was on his hands and knees before it, alter-  nately blowing the flame and fanning it with his hat. A paper of salt lay open on a stone beside the fire, but I thought, judging from the look of the fire and of the corn in his pail, that he would not need that seasoning for several hours to come.

I regarded this fellow wanderer with the mixed feel-ings of admiration and disdain that an amateur always has in the presence of a 'professional.' He worked at my play. He too was seeing Connecticut on foot like a gentleman, carrying his few needments on his back and thinking his own thoughts as he went along, keep-ing the twentieth century in its place; but somehow the consideration that he did nothing else all the year round took off the glamour. Doubtless he did it much

better than I. There were many rents in his coat, and
I had but one, very recently acquired. He was not
deeply concerned about his night's lodging, although
he seemed genuinely grateful when I told him that
there was an abandoned house round the bend of the
lane with two good windows in it. He did not burden
himself even with raisins and walnuts in a paper
envelope, as I did, but 'what he thought he might re-
quire he went and took.'

In all this he beat me at my own game; yet I was
not ashamed. I might have foraged about until I
found a few ears of corn for myself, brought them back
and begged that they might be boiled with his, and then,
while I shared his salt, I might have furbished my few
words of hobo vocabulary while absorbing many things
that are good to know about the lore of the road. But
then, to be consistent, should I not have gone on with
him after the supper fire was out and shared the deserted house in the woods, with the two good windows?
— supposing that he would abandon his unhoused free
condition for such a shelter. For aught I knew, he
might be headed for Wales or Holland. And so it
seemed best to preserve my amateur standing, although I was very hungry and the little fire had a
friendly though pathetic look just then, with the stars
beginning to peep. He did not know the road to Stafford
Springs, though I judged from what he said that he had
just come from there. One town was much the same
as another to him, and he did not clutter his memory
with names. . . . When I left him he was still blowing

at the fire. The water in his pail was as cold, I found by dipping a finger, as it could have been in the brook.

For another hour I plodded on through the gathering gloom, taking an indefinite number of turnings by little more than guesswork, though I knew that Stafford Springs must lie somewhere to the southwest, and when the sun was gone there were still the constellations to steer by. It was dismal work, with never a human sight or sound to break the loneliness, but now and then the guttural voice of a brook or a whisper of aspens, and once the weird clamor of a hoot-owl beating his rounds. . . . Then, suddenly, from a darkling hill to the left of my road, I heard the bleat of a sheep, and another, and a frightened scampering of little hooves. Moving on for a hundred yards, I found the small flock huddled about a gate to watch me go by, standing very still. Their mere presence in that wild place, twenty dim figures in the darkness, was strangely comforting. They seemed to be on my side, for I could feel that they were lonely too. They helped to humanize the ghostly whispering road, and lent a touch of antiquity to the Connecticut woods. For so many thousands of years men have been lying out at night with their sheep that now the slow return of the flocks into Connecticut seems to unite the country with times long gone by and with the Mesopotamian hills.

I moved on again. The ghosts came nearer. I could think of nothing but supper and bed. I envied the tramp his hard and half-warmed corn and the dry level

flooring of the abandoned house where he would sleep
that night with a roof above him, and perhaps an arm-
ful of clean straw for an added luxury. Still I plodded
onward, keeping the Great Bear pretty steadily at my
back.

Just as I was estimating the number of miles I had
walked that day since leaving Fairford — the final
stage of weakness in a rambler — I saw a pale glimmer
of light on the leaves overhead. The light grew; it
flooded the road and drew my gigantic shadow on the
gravel. I heard the purr of a powerful machine pad-
ding cat-footed behind me, and stood to one side among
the fern.

'Should you like to ride?' said, or rather sang, a
woman's voice as the car slowed to a stop.

'If you are going anywhere near Stafford Springs,'
I replied, 'I should be very glad to.'

'I'm going right there,' the voice sang again.

I climbed into the car and sank down upon the
cushions without a word. A walker, of course, would
not have done so, and a professional tramp might not
have had the chance. I was glad that I had preserved
my amateur standing.

My respect for the woman who picked me up on that
lonely road and took me not only to Stafford Springs
but five or six miles beyond, because she heard me express a vague wish for a familiar lodging, is equaled
only by my gratitude. I could not see her face in the
dim light of the car, and we said little during our ride
together, but her action showed that she was both fear-

less and kind. She saw that I was tired, and acted in the spirit of pure chivalry, which need not be the special prerogative of either sex. May grace attend her!

That night I slept in Tolland.

THE FLOCK AT EVENING

SUNSET is golden on the steep,
   And all our little valleys lie
Golden and still and full of sleep
   To watch the flocks go by.
Down through the winding leaf-hung lane,
Now blurred in shade, now bright again,
They trail in splendor, aureoled
And mystical in clouded gold.

As insubstantial as a dream
   They huddle homeward past my door . . .
From what Theocritean stream,
   Or what Thessalian shore?
An ancient air surrounds them still,
As though from some Arcadian hill
They shuffled through the afterglow
Across the fields of long ago.

Is this the flock Apollo kept
   From straying by his reed-soft tunes
While the long ilex shadow crept
   Through ancient afternoons?
In some dim legendary wood,
Ages ago, have these not stood
Wondering, circle-wise and mute,
Round some remote Sicilian flute?

I think that they have gazed across
　　The dazzle of Ionian seas
From the green capes of Tenedos
　　Or wave-washed Cyclades,
And wandered through the twilight down
The hills that gird some Attic town
Dim-shining in the purple gloam
Beside the whispering of pale foam.

What dream is this? I know the croft,
　　Deep in this vale, where they were born;
I know their wind-swept fields aloft
　　Among the waving corn.
Yet, while they glimmer slowly by,
A fairer earth and earlier sky
Seem round them, and they move sublime
Among the dews of dawning time.

VII

BY LITTLE RIVERS

Laudato si, misignore, per sor aqua,
La quale è multo utile et humele et pretiosa et casta.
— SAINT FRANCIS OF ASSISI

The God of Nature hath not discovered himself so variously won-
derful in anything as in the waters of fountains, rivers and streams.
— THOMAS FULLER

 CONSIDERING its station on a granite hill, Tolland is a remarkably streamy town, 'like Jason's fleece, irriguous with a dew from heaven when much of the vicinage is dry.' Perhaps because I have so often gone there for the April fishing — with my strong and quiet friend who now casts his flies, alas! over celestial pools — I never find myself in Tolland, or even hear its name spoken without giving thanks for its great store of water-brooks. Wherever a man walks in that township, he is never long without the chuckle of a brook or the gurgling of some rivulet beside him, or else the smooth strong gliding of the Skungamaug. Tolland sits like Peele's Bathsheba 'within the hearing of a thousand streams,' so that all day long, and more clearly in the night, you may hear there, beneath the pour of wind through her high-uplifted elms and ma-

ples, a noise of water falling, a song of water rippling, or the silken whisper of water sweetly flowing to the sea.

When I awoke at my friendly inn I remembered these things, and I thought of a dozen watercourses that would be singing welcome on that morning of September shine. Seeing that I had set myself to walk straight across the northern boundary of Connecticut and that I lay here a good ten miles to the south of that line, it seemed appropriate that I should spend this day in calling upon certain streams of my more intimate acquaintance. . . . For I need hardly say that a main advantage in making a settled plan for such a ramble as mine is that one then has something to depart from and to defy, with a vaguely pleasant sense of guilt.

Just down the long hill that slopes from the Tolland inn, there is a nameless brook that bursts out of an alder thicket into a little pine grove, and there, beneath the pines, some one has made a clearing and placed a bench. Before the last shreds of morning mist had lifted from the meadows I was seated in this place, watching the dance of waves and the feathering of white water over diminutive falls. All morning long I sat there, in happy idleness. Of course this was not keeping the agreement I had made with myself, but all the excuse I need may be found in the words of Emerson's 'Apology':

> Tax me not with sloth that I
> Fold my arms beside the brook:
> Each cloud that floated in the sky
> Writes a letter in my book.

It is strange how little has been adequately written about American streams. When Thoreau said that the splendid stains of the American October have hardly tinged our poetry he might have gone on to say that the free cadenzas of brook-song have not been echoed in the rhythms of our prose. Latterly, of course, we have grown shame-faced about all song, and afraid of showing delight in anything so simple, obvious, and hackneyed as a brook. But this particular phase of æsthetic adolescence has not always been upon us and, God helping us, it may not last forever. We may yet come to see that almost the only things worth writing about are the hackneyed, obvious, and simple things; and if we ever do attain that degree of æsthetic maturity we shall see that running water is a worthy subject for any man's pen.

Just here, however, it occurs to me that a large part of what I know about streams was acquired not by sitting idly on the banks and watching the water dance by me but rather by clambering, leaping, splashing, and falling in the water itself, trout-rod in hand and creel on back. And it seems proper, therefore, that I should begin my pæan to little rivers with a prelude upon trout-fishing.

READER — What! In September! When does the trout season end?

WRITER — During the trout season one fishes. For the rest of the year one dreams and writes about trout-fishing.

READER — Isn't it a rather old topic?

WRITER — All the topics in this book are old topics.
READER — O, well . . .

There is a well-known disease which has not been
listed by the pathologists, an annual fever that sets in

with special virulence in
most States of the Union
about the first of April.
The symptoms of this dis-
ease, *febris salmonalis*, are
widely familiar. The pa-
tient — if that name may
be given one whose whole
complaint consists of im-
patience—dreams by night
and day of shining reels
and of bamboo rods bent double, of shadowy pools
where rhododendrons toss in the breeze, and of bright
stretches of dancing water, of gaudy feathers suddenly sucked out of the sunlight under dripping ledges.
He hears the guttural song of streams; he feels along
his arm and down his spine the tug of a sudden circling weight; he suffers with illusions of grandeur; red
spots on a brown and silvery ground dance before
his eyes. These and other such pictures get between
him and his newspaper. Or he may be sitting in his
office and thinking only of business when all at once,
as though his brain were a movie screen, the desk, the
papers on it, even the stenographer before him, fade
slowly out, and he sees himself standing knee-deep in a

rapid river, his straining rod held high in one hand while his net is pushed far forward by the other toward a gleaming shape that flounders and sidles toward him through the riffle.

It is said that we are a lawless people; we say it ourselves; but however that may be, you will find no true sportsman by even the loneliest stream earlier than one hour before sunrise on the opening day. No one is more keenly aware than the angler that the law is a brutally rigid and irrational thing, and no one knows better than he how widely the seasons vary from year to year, the first of March in some years being the equivalent of the first of May in some others. Yet he conforms, and is a shining example of the triumph of law not merely over reason but over primal instinct.

It is not the fear that others will take all the fish that gets the enthusiast out as early as the law allows. If that were all, he would remain at home when his practiced eye tells him that the weather is inauspicious. For he is a cheerful fatalist. To the list of Emerson's Spiritual Laws he would add one more item, viz: 'He shall catch his own trout. All that are meant for him radiate toward his angle by eternal laws.' Or he might quote John Burroughs's paraphrase of Emerson:

> Serene I fold my hands and wait,
> For lo! my own shall come to me.

No indecent haste to catch the trout that must eventually find their way into his basket draws him forth, but partly the natural desire to visit familiar scenes. Of these every fisherman has a list of his own. I should like to see a certain emerald pool, almost a perfect bowl of granite, ten feet across and twenty deep. There were never any trout in this pool, but there was always a marvel of color. I should also like to see again a certain sunken log under which my last Parmacheenee Belle suddenly vanished one April afternoon long ago and never came back. Most of all, I should like once more to let out a hundred feet of line over a certain dangerous cliff and into the wellnigh inaccessible virgin waters beneath, out of which there came, years since, a Gargantuan tug. What sort of trout might inhabit that chasm, into which it seemed unlikely that any man had ever thrown a line before? I could form no kind of guess, for I could not see the water, and even its mighty roar was vague with distance. It must suffice to say that no trout had ever made so tremendous a lunge at any tackle of mine before, and that none has ever done so since.

With only a few feet of unused line on which to play a large fish and with an extremely light rod whereby to lift I could not say how many jerking pounds, there was only one thing to do. I did it with groaning and anguish of spirit. Hooking one ankle about a root of arbor-vitæ to save myself from slipping down the smooth wet granite into the gorge, I laid the rod aside and began drawing in the line hand-over-hand, dragging it over a sharp edge of rock that hid from me both water and fish. (I do not pretend that this was high piscatorial art, but I know that it was exciting; and

even to-day, after years of meditation, I fail to see how
I could have acted much more wisely than I did.)

The oiled silk held nobly and the great trout wearied
little by little during his long ascent — surely as startling an experience as any trout ever knew. At last —
oh, at long last! — the line was all drawn in. I saw the
knot that held the six-foot gut leader. And then I suddenly remembered with startling vividness that the
leader was frayed and worn toward the lower end. I
could see just how it had looked when I tossed it over
into the chasm. Would it hold? Could it stand the
cruel strain of the final pull over that granite edge,
when the trout would be aroused by the touch of the
stone to frenzied activity? There was no way of swinging him free of that edge, for it was fifteen feet beyond
my farthest reach. Ages came and went. I can see to
this hour the grain of the sloping rock on which I
crouched and the mossy crevice by which my forward
foot was supported. I can hear the cry of the canyon
wind in the cedar overhead, and the louder cry of the
hidden water below. This indelible picture of the mind
was made by instantaneous exposure while the fish was
dangling just below me, still out of sight. That last
agonizing pull had to be made. . . . It was made — and
within six inches of victory the leader snapped in two
and the most majestic of all created trout dropped back
into freedom. We never saw each other.

Most fishermen have acquired a few finny friends,
and these also must be visited early in the season, for
one feels a not wholly disinterested anxiety about their

health, and wants to know how they have come through the winter. I shall long remember one of these acquaintances, a trout of noble inches who had all to himself a large pool in the California mountains. Season after season I had gone up against him and had tried him with every wile I knew, including that of the grasshopper. Often I made little trips to his pool without rod or tackle just to make sure that he was still there, so that I grew familiar with his daily routine and came to think of him as mine. My interest in his welfare was whetted somewhat, of course, by natural curiosity as to whether he was one of the elect or whether he was to be damned to some other man's basket.

The question was most rudely answered. On a certain first of April I arrived punctually at his pool, accompanied by a friend to whom I had incautiously confided the secret. I fished the pool with great care, but unsuccessfully, for half an hour, while my friend went on to the pool above. Suddenly I heard a shout and a crashing in the bushes, and, looking up, saw my friend standing by the waterfall above me and holding up my trout, the large purple eyes already glazing, unmistakably and merely a corpse. I do not know whether it should be admitted that I ate a part of this trout an hour later at breakfast, and that he tasted very good. During the years of our acquaintance he had come to seem to me almost a person, and now he appeared before me in a very novel form, neatly halved and delicately browned on a pine plank. In that early meal

under the live-oak I had a faint reminiscence of the
forgotten joys of cannibalism.

However it may be with other sportsmen, the angler
for trout is chiefly engaged in the collection of pleasant
memories. The closed season is just long enough for
the torture of black flies and mosquitoes, for the mis-
eries of the alder-brake where one's line snarls at every
turn, for the weariness of the long tramp homeward
with water-soaked boots, to fade out of memory. The
enthusiast can remember many an empty creel, but
never an empty fishing day, for he casts his flies into
beauty and draws them back over the waters of peace.
Though he may take no fish, though the total result
of his day's labor may remind him forcibly of the
Apostle's definition of Faith, it will be his own fault
if he does not bring home at least a sabbath calm of
body and mind and soul.

It must be that I am losing my talent for idleness,
else I should not have been troubled by the thought
that several million men within a hundred miles of me
were engaged in tasks at least ostensibly useful during
the hours I dreamed away beside Nameless Brook. I
knew that all that while they had been scurrying busily
here and there like so many ants, transferring matter
from spot to spot, digging holes and filling them up
again, collecting metal disks and bits of written paper
into piles. I could almost see their eager purposeful
faces as they scampered up and down the runways and
galleries of the gigantic ant-hill to the south. How

could a mere rambler justify himself against all that multitude of severely practical hole-fillers and disk-collectors? Their very number seemed a cogent argu-ment in their favor, for a good American must of course believe that the majority is always right; and I knew, besides, that they had a stern conviction of their rectitude such as a rambler seldom feels about himself.

In a world in which the rambler is but one in the million he does well to look about for some sort of protective coloration. How, then, could I give my morning beside the stream any semblance of social value? Well, it occurred to me that not every one has ever seen a brook in a full and effective sense. Those millions of sternly practical men, for example, did not act as though they had ever seen one, and I thought that a long deep gaze into a woodland brook such as this before me would do some of them some kind of good. So I pulled out my note-book and set down the random jottings in stream lore that follow. It was a naïve notion, certainly, for an idle man to set himself the task of addressing Wall Street on the topic of brooks, and it illustrates once more the fact that when one is determined to write he will invent astonishing excuses. . . . But here are my notes:

A little stream, six or seven feet in width and not more than ten inches deep in most places, flows down before me through a glade of pines, coming out of a clearing just visible through the dark stems above and

going down into another. There is deep shadow, of the peculiarly lustrous and richly colored kind that only pines can throw, upon most of its course, and this shadow is darkest on the glossy pool some thirty feet up the stream, but elsewhere the sunlight dazzles in patches upon white water. The banks on either side are purple with pine needles. A rod or two up the water there is a foot-bridge of two mouldering planks, and beyond that a fence of sagging wire to separate the glade from the clearing.

In this rough outline there is nothing much to excite attention. Nearly all the values lie in minute details, as they must in landscapes drawn to so small a scale, and for this reason, precisely, the forest brook provides the best possible education for the eye. There is always more to be seen in it than any one has yet seen. A man may gaze at a small patch of stream-surface until he thinks he has exhausted every trait of motion, shape, and hue; then he looks again, and finds that he has just begun to spell out its primer. Not that a brook ever tries to hide anything, for there is nothing more frank and generous in self-revelation; but its carvings are so many and its nuances of color so fine, its endless dance is so full of what looks like pure whim and caprice, that it daunts and finally eludes the most patient skill of the eye. One who has learned to see a brook can see anything.

A painter of the modern schools would represent the stream as simply as possible, noting down first of all the supple bending of the banks and recording the vivid contrasts of gleam and gloom. But he would actually see far more than this, finding between the extremes of shade and shine a whole gamut of lighting, of steely glitter and soft translucence, of colors nameless and numberless reflected from the sky and the boughs or striking upward from the pebbled bed. Between the pool and the waterfall are innumerable gradations of eddy and curve and rapid, of shaded

whorls and sunlit dimplings, of glitter on a sable
ground, of wavelets pouting like a Naiad's breasts or
dinted like the moulds that formed them. One begins
to see the brook accurately, and so to discover the true
beauty of running water, only when he learns that it
is wonderfully various, that it is reticulated and scored
into minute and ever minuter subdivisions that finally
go beyond the power of any eye and are seen by the
fancy only, by an imagination half poetical and half
scientific.

But the impressionistic painter would be quite justi-
fied in attending chiefly to the more obvious aspects of
the brook scenery, not only because these are all that
he can hope to represent but also because the effects of
running water, almost infinitely various as a close examination finds them to be, are composed of a few
fundamental forms: the standing pool, slow water, the
slide, the rapid, the eddy, the curve, and the fall. The
whole dance of the brook is based upon these ever-
recurring patterns, all of which may be found in almost
any hundred yards of water. Thus, after we have
learned that what seemed at first so simple is unthink-
ably intricate, we may go on to learn that what seems
so intricate is really simple after all.

Much the same final lesson is taught by the stream
of life to those who study it deeply enough. Two kinds
of men see that stream as simple: wise men and fools;
but the simplicity that wise men discover is very different from that which fools imagine. Only those who
are well-informed and at the same time half-educated,

being neither deeply wise nor yet quite foolish, continue long in the elementary belief that our life is essentially multiple and miscellaneous. A single year of time, closely watched, should teach them better, just as a hundred yards of the stream is enough for one who can use his eyes. The naïve opinion that wisdom grows only with knowledge and experience, so that only old men can be deeply wise, has no more justification than the belief that in order to understand this brook before me I should have to follow it clear to its mouth. That would be the way to unlearn and to forget the little that I have found out, as old men so commonly do. The young man, not infrequently, is wiser than his father because he is not bewildered by the apparent multiplicity of life. Birth and death, mourning and festival, love and hate, ambition and failure — these and a few more are the recurring forms and patterns to be found in the stream of life, and it does not take long to learn them. Even these we may come to see as negligible phases of one vast unitary flow out of the Deep and down again into the Great Deep.

The pool, slow water, the slide, the rapid, the eddy, the curve, and the fall — there is the alphabet of streams, in which all their endless literature is written. In every rod of the brook I find elements that I have seen a thousand times before, yet they have always some touch of novelty in their arrangement. No two pools are ever exactly alike, and no two eddies or waterfalls. Like my own life, the stream says the same

thing over and over without ever repeating itself, and
I think I could listen to it forever. Line upon line
and precept upon precept —
it is an excellent teacher.
More than any other thing
I know it gives us the delight of discovering unity in
the midst of variety. No-
where else, I think, does the
One hide itself so transpar-
ently behind the changing
Many. It has been truly
said that we can never

bathe twice in the same stream, and yet, in another
sense, the stream remains forever the same. As the
poet Quevedo saw, standing by the Tiber and comparing its ageless current with the ruins of Rome
about him, 'only the fugitive is permanent.' No stream
can ever grow old. Humanity is doomed, with all of
its proudest works; the hills stand a little lower after
every summer rain; the mountains are crumbling hour
by hour; but the stream that twirls them down and
buries them all at sea laughs and sings as blithely at
its task to-day as it did on creation's morning. Without either haste or rest, it carries them all away. The
stream is the oldest thing we know, and the youngest
as well. It has no age. It is time racing down forever
through the channels of eternity.

Waves of the sea and of rivers constantly shift from
place to place because they are not controlled by solid

bodies of earth or rock, but the ridges and hollows of the brook's surface — which do not exactly correspond, to be sure, to the waves of larger bodies of water — are stable without being rigid. These hollows and hummocks, whorls and parabolas and serpentine curves are constantly wavering, but they remain essentially unchanged from hour to hour and from day to day. They may even disappear for a moment, but they return again inevitably, like the recurring themes of music. While the volume of water and the shape of the bed and banks remain what they are, these also remain, as though they were cut in granite or bronze. In some lights and at a certain distance the brook seems to be made of carven metal, upon which the only moving thing is the slowly unraveling foam.

Even from where I sit, close to the bank, the water seems now and then to be standing still, as though suddenly congealed. I can see the threads and skeins of water-drops coming over the fall, and there is a constant vibration or trembling over the entire surface, but these things alone would not suggest a downward motion. Only the bubbles that float so bravely out into the pool convey a suggestion of the current. They come toward me round the bend in stately companies, sailing serenely, with all the sky upon them,

> Under the green and golden atmosphere
> Which noontide kindles through the woven leaves.

They set forth in gallant argosies as though bound on some high adventure — but they always burst before they have gone a dozen feet.

The most beautiful thing about a brook is its liberty, by which grossly misused word I choose to mean nothing like license but willing subjection to a law that is self-imposed. Casually glanced at, the stream may appear to splash and sprawl quite recklessly, like a libertine; but nothing in Nature is so lawless as romantic poets would have us believe, and least of all a stream. Look again, look more deeply, and you will find that in every ripple perfect spontaneity is wonderfully married to routine. The rhythms of the brook may seem to be irregular, like those of a modern lyric, but that is only because we do not know the laws of their periodicity. Even the apparent variations are regular. For half an hour I have wondered vaguely about a larger wave that creams from time to time quite over a rock in the stream-bed which stands at other times above the surface, but just now I have discovered that this inundation occurs at regular intervals of about twenty seconds. Thus the stream is ruled in every part by laws conformable to its nature which it has made its own, and so it is really free. It is like a great improviser who expresses himself spontaneously within the laws of an intricate counterpoint.

I cannot say whether it is partly because of the stream's subtle and half-glimpsed analogies with human life that I am always happy near running water and gravitate inevitably to the bottom of every little valley where a brook is flowing. Its mingling of form and color with motion, and the addition to these of endless song, would account for much of my delight, but I think the real cause lies deeper. The brook moves in rhythm, like music and poetry and dance, and it recalls these arts that we have devised to express the inexpressible. The water seems to be going my way; I lock step with its onward march; its pulse and my heart-beat are one, its rhythm and my breath. It shares with me one origin and destiny. I know how gladly it would linger in the sunny pool, but I know also that it is drawn downward to the great sea by a deeper fascination. For I am a single drop of water in the stream, or one of the myriad bubbles that set out so bravely toward eternity and burst before they have well started — yet I think they all arrive somehow at their goal. The bubble bursts and the drop is merged forever with the element; but the stream itself, and the forms and shapes the water wears, endure. The drops that swirled past me when I first came here are now miles away, but the volume and shape of the stream are still the same. The wrinkle of crystal water at the foot of yonder rock has not vanished for an instant. Such bubbles as those below the fall may have swarmed and swum and winked there since before the carving of the Sphinx. They may wink and swim and swarm there until the pyramids are worn to the level of the desert sand.

Deep in the afternoon, when shadows were lengthening eastward and the sun-glint was striking upward among the leaves from the ripples of the little Skungamaug, I came in my walk to a cove of rocks beside the stream and sat down there under the sweep of wild apple boughs. Just at my feet the water slipped swiftly by, going down a long and mossy slide into the sunlit pool below with a multitudinous gurgle and shout of innumerable voices. Upon the current were sailing here a yellow leaf of alder and there a curled gray leaf of willow, and the waves that sustained these tiny skiffs were topaz, amber, or maroon, according as the rocks over which they ran varied in hue or as the sunlight struck them. The apple leaves above, already sparse and yellowing, swayed to and fro, up and down, in a long draught of air that moved like an unseen river down the valley. Every other voice was shut away by the voice of the stream as by a closed door, so that I sat in a little solitude of sound. The stream and I were alone together.

By the side of running water my thoughts, if I think at all, are borne away on the waves, leaving me with no measure of time. The minutes grow imperceptibly into hours, so that when I come to leave I take with me no definite memories, no deepened wisdom, only a vague sense that I have been happy. On this afternoon, however, I was to have better fortune.

A sound very different from the sound of the stream broke suddenly in upon the tumultuous privacy that the racing waters had piled about my lair. It was a quick whirr of tiny wings, very near at hand. Instantly I knew what caused it and whence it came. I raised my eyes without turning my head. Five feet from me, delicately poised in a sunbeam, was that winged emerald, child of light and air, that we call with utter inadequacy a humming-bird. For only a second

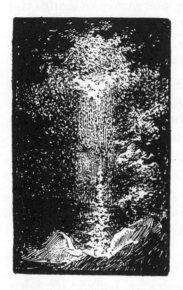

he trod the air before me, his wings weaving a nimbus of glory about his head, but in that second my eye met his, a microscopic bead of deepest jet, the wildest thing and the most vividly alert that I have ever seen.

Satisfied by his scrutiny of the intruder, he darted two feet to the left, and there floated again, his wings still winnowing the air and his head borne proudly aloft. He was now engaged on business, for before him stood the tall swaying spike of a cardinal flower. How I had failed to see this blaze of color during all the time I had sat there I do not know, for when my visitor pointed it out with his needle bill it was all aflame in full sunshine. With his feathers glistening like green metal and his ruby crest flaming in unison with the flower, he seemed the very genius of the scene.

Less than ten seconds, perhaps no more than five, he hovered beside the cardinal flower, sipping a delicate draught from each of its gorgeous flagons. Then he flashed across the water on a beam of light, and was gone.

His going was like the close of perfect music. In imagination, I saw his tiny body hurtling by over the tree-tops at twice the speed of an express train, as often I have seen those of his kind in California, and I longed to know how to call him back. Never have I felt more poignantly the pathos of beauty's sudden incursions into our days and the mystery of her swift departures. Would it not have been better, I asked myself, if the bird had not come at all?

And yet I knew, and know, that five such seconds are enough to illumine a day, a week, or many months, to one who can remember. They are enough to redeem all a man's years from hopeless groping and groveling, for they may serve to remind him always that perfection must somewhere exist because he has seen it once.

The voice of the stream came back to me after the bird was gone with a deeper meaning, and the sunlight fell through the shifting leaves as it did when I was a child. The dragon-fly steering up and down on his mysterious errands was my friendly fellow-guest, and the leaves voyaging through shadow and gleam to the sea were my companions on one and the same vast journey. Most of all the cardinal flower retained the glamour of the bird's presence. Tall and proud in its sunbeam, swaying a little in the wind, it stood forth against the gray-blue rocks and shaded fern like a vivid gleed. The total wealth of summer was focussed for me by this final culminating blossom. It drew the eve like a single lamp in a dark landscape.

Nothing could have been added to that moment beside the stream that would have made it a more perfect assurance of the beauty that shines, I know, through all things, but is not often so clearly seen. It was as though a door had opened, letting glory through. The door closed; but still I can remember. To a man who has had only one such glimpse into perfection the poets and saints and mystics need never again seem to babble in an utterly unknown tongue.

VIII

SOLITUDE AND MULTITUDE

And Wisdom's self
Oft seeks to sweet retirèd solitude,
Where, with her best nurse, Contemplation,
She plumes her feathers, and lets grow her wings,
That, in the various bustle of resort,
Were all to-ruffled, and sometimes impaired.

— MILTON

 I ALLOWED the automobile to undo what the automobile had done by riding back into the town of Stafford with mine host of the Tolland Inn. Whether I began to walk at the precise spot at which I had left off thirty-six hours before is nothing to the purpose, for a rambler is not driven by his conscience. Neither do I think it necessary to enlarge upon the ancient fame of Stafford Springs as a spa, for that glory is departed.

I have nothing against the citizens of Stafford themselves except that there are too many of them. In 1810 there were already more than two thousand, and the intervening years have added heaven and the census-taker know how many more. For this reason I found myself early in the morning two miles from the town — at Orcuttsville, to be exact and cacophanous — engaged upon the major problem of the rambler in these days of macadam, how to avoid the highway. Every one in Orcuttsville — that is to say, the man who kept the filling-station and his wife and his mother-in-law and his little boy — when asked about the road to Windsor Locks, pointed down the straight hard smooth thoroughfare along which, on that Sunday morning, the blue breath of the automobile was already lying in noxious layers. I told Orcuttsville that I wished to walk, although, considering my appearance, the explanation seemed to me superfluous. Well, that was the road to walk on. But was there no aged, decrepit, and good-for-nothing road, no winding and rutty and almost abandoned lane with a dirt surface and grass growing between the wheel-tracks, that would take me in a westerly direction until I came to the River? Oh, yes, they said, with smiles half pitying and half indulgent; yes, there was some such road as that up north a piece, round Crow Hill way, but they had forgotten just where. They wanted me to understand, however, that this northern road was 'awful rough, and all up and down, as you might say, and lonesome,' and that if I wanted to get to Windsor Locks by night I had better take the main thoroughfare running westward. By going that way I might 'catch a lift.' So I went north. The road that Orcuttsville had forgotten was the road for me.

There is no better example in the world of the law of compensation than that provided by the roads of New England considered from the rambler's point of view.

The highway, to be sure, is obnoxious to his foot, eye, ear, and nose, but the highway cannot be everywhere. It sucks into its channel nearly all the traffic that once flowed along a dozen others, and therefore, while it grows 'better' year by year, a dozen roads that run in the same general direction are growing delightfully worse. For every inch of crushed stone added to its surface we may reasonably suppose that a corresponding inch is added to the depth of their ruts. For every foot by which its gravel shoulders are widened, the boughs of ash and elm lean a foot farther over the roads of yesteryear. The highway draws all the billboards to itself and so leaves the little roads undesecrated; it keeps to itself the scream of brakes and

the griding of claxons, and so it is still possible to hear in New England the song of the woodthrush and the whitethroated sparrow. The automobile has made New England a pedestrian's paradise.

Nowhere does the sunshine lie more golden, blurred and blotted by swift shadows, than in one of these old ways 'paved with afternoon' that come from no particular place and go by roundabout routes nowhither. By following one of them for a mile one may learn what Stevenson meant in saying that it is a better thing to travel hopefully than to arrive, for beyond every bend there is a lurking mystery and a romantic distance to lure us on and on. And it is not as though men had carelessly let them escape; rather, they have run away, as I was doing. The road before me brought to mind, somehow, that glorious defiance of Coriolanus to the Roman mob: 'You common cry of curs . . . I banish *you!*' Only my road was no longer defiant; it had simply forgotten the ways of men, and taught me to do the same.

Thinking of these things, I sat down under a sycamore three miles from Orcuttsville and addressed my holiday companion in appropriate verses:

AN ABANDONED ROAD

Down from the windy and sun-washed hill,
  Down through the maple glade,
Down where the aspen leaf is still,
  It sinks to a moted shade:
And there, stretched out in glad release,
  It lapses, blurred and blind,
Into the infinite lonely peace
  Of things gone out of mind.

Shadows are shifting upon the moss
  That covers the wagon-track;
Spiders are weaving their webs across,
  And gossamers floating slack;
And all the winds have whispered away
  From the sequestered wood,
Leaving to Silence her ancient sway
  In a green solitude.

Only the voice of a hermit thrush
Deep-hidden in leafy Junes
Ripples the lake of this breathless hush
Through lingering afternoons;
And no step moves here all day through,
And no man lives who knows
Out of what valleys it comes or to
What purple hills it goes.

Only a rambler with heart washed clear
Of sorrow and old regrets
Lingers alone in the quiet here
On the road that the world forgets . . .
And follows it, loitering, down the glen
Dim-bannered with goldenrod,
Out of the thoughts and the needs of men
Wandering back to God.

Straight north from Orcuttsville ran my road, deteriorating with gratifying rapidity as it went, so that I feared it might dodge away into Massachusetts and leave me. All it meant, however, was to get round Crow Hill, and when it had done this, skirting the very boundary line of the northern state as a skater does a hole in the ice, it snuggled down into Connecticut again, making for the gap between Bald and Soapstone mountains. The five-mile tramp toward that gap lay through unbroken woodland. I met on the way several families going to church, one hermit who was knocking apples out of a tree above his shack, a man and woman engaged in admiration of the landscape, and a small boy driving a cow. All of these people — a surprising number to find at such a place and time — were foreigners in one sense or another. At last, however, I encountered a native, a specimen of that noble but rapidly disappearing species which should be known as *Homo Connecticutensis*, standing before the door of his house on the loneliest stretch of that lonely road.

He was a man of middle age, well read and well spoken, a college graduate, who had always lived in this house, which he said was the oldest inhabited house in Tolland County, except for the years of his schooling. With him I had some good talk about solitude, upon which topic I expected to find him an expert, considering that his little farm was beleaguered by the forest and that his nearest neighbor lived a mile away. Unlike the patriarch of North Ashford, he

knew the meaning of solitude and admitted the knowledge; but like most sensible men who have had long experience of loneliness, he did not much enjoy it — or perhaps he thought that half a lifetime of it was an overdose. We quoted some of the *loci classici* on the subject, beginning with Scipio's hackneyed '*Numquam minus solus quam solus*' and coming down to

Thoreau's 'I have never yet found the companion who is so companionable as solitude.' Most of these remarks, we agreed, were only egoism masquerading as philosophy, and few of them were uttered by men who had earned the right to speak. I gave him the gist of a passage from the letters of Thoreau which he had never met with: 'It is not that we love to be alone, but that we love to soar, and when we do soar the company grows thinner and thinner till there is none at all. We are not the less to aim at the summits, though the multitude does not ascend them. Use all the society that will abet you.' This he thought was good sense, and we agreed that Thoreau often showed good sense when he was not striking attitudes and trying to make people gasp. One convincing proof, I said, that most amateurs of the solitary life — excepting certain hermits of the Thebaïd — have not known what they are talking about is that they never mention the terror of solitude, as I had felt it more than once in broad daylight on the tops of the California mountains. He looked at me strangely when I said this, as though he thought, 'So you have known that too!' But he did not say that he had.

Just after the road I was traveling crosses the townline of Somers, it comes to the fern-and-hemlock-covered ledges of Bald Mountain, a granite eminence some twelve hundred feet in height. Having walked for several miles along leafy lanes, I thought the view from this mountain would add an agreeable variety to

the day's travel, and I decided to climb the slope. Half
a mile of scrambling among the laurel bushes brought
me to the summit. There I saw the counties stretching
themselves in the sun on every side, colored with that
same sunny green that had delighted me in the tiny
map I studied in New York; and running down between them was the pale blue ribbon of the River. It
was as though that little map, four inches wide by two
and a half in depth, were suddenly realized before
me, magnified by several
million diameters. Al-
though my altitude had
been rather easily won,
I was really high up
in the only sense that
counts, for no neighbor-
ing hill stood higher than
mine. Westward I looked
to Talcott Mountain and
its tower, twenty miles
away, and over that to
the heights of Salisbury
whither I was bound.
Southward, beyond the
dome of Soapstone

Mountain, lay the Sound, hidden by fifty miles of distance. Eastward were the hills of Union where I had
wandered and lost my way two days before. (Under
which of them, I wondered, was my fellow-rambler
trying to boil his corn this bright noon-day?) And far

off to northward, in the foreign land of Massachusetts, Mounts Tom and Holyoke stood up and took the sunshine. We were an exalted company.

I ate my luncheon there while I walked about, and left a few nuts and raisins for any squirrel that might climb so high; then I found a granite seat, rested my back against a stump of arbor-vitæ, faced southward toward Connecticut, found my notebook and pencil, and . . .

READER — I pray Heaven you are not going to write a description!

WRITER — Why not?

READER — First, because I don't think I can stand it; and second, because you said you had sworn a great oath not to.

WRITER — Firstly, then, you may skip it; and secondly, when I swore that oath I did not remember having climbed Bald Mountain. . . .

As I was saying, I found my notebook and pencil. Then I wrote the following note or memorandum, which may as well be left in the present tense:

There is not a breath of moving air in all the sky. Except for the leaves of a slender poplar halfway down the hill, which seem to move by an inward propulsion, all the foliage hangs inert. Not a bough is waving. The pod of milkweed at my side has not launched one of its thousand airships while I have sat here, and the shallop of dandelion-tuft glistening high overhead seems becalmed. Heat waves shimmer above the ground. Six or seven late butterflies flap aimlessly about, or bask with slowly opening and closing wings upon a sunny stump.

A few clouds hang low on the eastern horizon, seeming rather to increase than to diminish the day's brimming light, their shapeless shadows sprawling beneath them as though painted on the hills. Vivid light spills from every quarter of the sky, and is reflected from every surface in flashing brilliancy. Light soaks into the fibers of the fallen trunk beside me; it bleaches the grass and the last year's leaves at my feet, taking back the color it lent; it triumphs everywhere, trampling upon the woods, the plain, the far-off hills. I feel that the planet itself is but a tiny sand-grain washed round and borne along in the torrent of overwhelming light.

Over and through all that I see there is woven an endless quiet — the quiet of the sky which earth's voices never interrupt. Now and then a goldfinch charges by, uttering his staccato warble at each downward plunge. A nuthatch, at work in the wood below me, calls at odd intervals in his nasal contralto. A cicada, wakened by the sun that feels like August, tears the seam of silence furiously at every third minute. Crickets are chirping all about, giving thanks in a hundred voices for a day entirely to their mind. Yet all these sounds serve only to punctuate the profound stillness. They are merely an overture to the great symphony of silence playing overhead in the spaces of the sky.

Now Earth has done her utmost, and takes a time for pause and quiet resting. There are grapes to ripen and gentians yet to come, with all the crashing coda of October gold and scarlet, but these will bring themselves to pass upon the momentum already gathered. This is Earth's day of attainment, her harvest-home; she is bringing in her sheaves. Even more, therefore, than at other times, there is in the air a tone of thrilling expectancy, as of some event unimaginably vast or of some tremendous word to which the long upward sweep of the year would be a fitting prelude. The stage is set. When will the play begin? What is it that the hills are waiting for? What do the poplars whisper among themselves? What secret does the sea rumble and roar out yonder in its outlandish tongue? For I think it is the sea that knows. The hills can only wait, like us; and they wear a look of having waited long.

A thousand feet above me two hawks are soaring. They move in opposed but interlocking circles that seem to diminish as they climb their spiral stair. Very slowly they drift northward, as though some lofty current of air were wafting them. From minute to minute they do not flap a wing, but draw their elaborate pattern against the sky in what seems an effortless floating. They tower to the outer verge of vision, and now I catch only an occasional glint from the under side of a wing as they wheel, as though a fleck of mica were falling from the blue. . . . At last they are blotted out, light absorbs them, and my eyes come back to watch a cricket climbing a grass stem.

A drowsy butterfly leaves his stump and flutters away haphazardly. Another goldfinch plunges past on some pressing errand, bounding up and down like a tiny dolphin of the air. Once more the cicada fills the noon with raucous clamor. Solitude, silence, and sunshine engulf me like the waves of a shoreless sea.

The village of Somers was asleep when I arrived there in the early afternoon, not having roused itself as yet from the morning sermon. The driver of the bus standing on the highway was asleep, and behind him sat one passenger, also asleep, waiting, I judged, for an early start on Monday morning. The proprietor of the hotel was asleep in the sun on his verandah, leaning back against a post with the newspaper open on his lap. In front of the hotel and in the very middle of the road lay a large black dog, asleep.

But I wanted to inquire about the way to North Somers, which was not shown on my map, for in that town, I had been told, they still speak Elizabethan English, use the flail and warming-pan, and cook by the open hearth. Not that I believed much of this, but still . . . At last I found an 'Ice Cream Parlor' that seemed to be open for business, and although I did not want to eat ice cream I entered and sat down, asking the slattern who served me to give me directions.

'Henry,' said she, 'you tell this fella the way to North Summers.'

Henry was slouching in a rocking-chair at one corner of the room, his stockinged feet upon another chair, engaged in a deliberate absorption of the Sunday Supplement which somehow reminded me of the feed-

ing-habits of the boa constrictor. Henry had not
shaved that Sunday morning or for several mornings
before, nor had he thought it worth his while to don
coat, collar, or cravat. Henry was taking his ease
after the week's labors. He removed his cold cigar
from his lips and said to the woman, without once
looking at me: 'They ain't no use tryin' to tell a fella
the way to North Summers who ain't never ben there.
You know yourself you gotta know the way or you
can't never find it. You gotta go down to Grimes's old
blacksmith shop and then up past Hackett's mill, and
cut through the woods a piece till you come to the
pond, and then you turn right and go on until you get
there. That's all. But they ain't no use tellin' a fella.'

With a look expressing both exhaustion and dis-
gust, Henry put the cold cigar back into his mouth as
though he were stopping a leak, and resumed his
deglutition of the comic page. There was an insolence
in his manner, or else a brutal stupidity, to which I
could find no adequate answer. I paid for the untasted
ice cream and walked out of the shop, closing the door
very softly. Friendship Valley seemed to have come
to an end.

The road to Windsor Locks, when it leaves Somers,
cuts through a corner of Ellington, which is a good
town and has the look of containing several civilized
people. All that I have to say about it may be said
in the words of the poet Edward Rowland Sill, who
wrote a letter in 1883, from his native Windsor, about

a walk he had just taken in that direction. 'There is
nothing but rye,' says he, 'in the sandy plains between here and Ellington — or a little tobacco and
spindly corn. Plain living and high thinking must be
the rule out along
there among the
farmers. Elling-
ton is beautiful.
It might be just
a little *quiet* in
winter, but at this
season it is great.
There's a glorious
silence there. I
saw a man and a

boy with a toy wagon, and another man, all on the
street at once. But they went into doorways and were
seen no more. What a dignity and placid reserve
about the place! The houses all look like the coun-
try-seats of persons of great respectability who had
retired on a competence — and retired a great ways
while they were about it. And what *big* houses they
used to build. *Used* to, I say, because there isn't a
house over there that looks less than a thousand years
old; not that they look old as seeming worn or rickety
but old as being very stately and wise and imperturb-
able.'

This passage shows what we might have expected,
that Sill had a delicate discernment for the charm of
little towns. It reminds me of another passage, written

much more recently by Dean Inge of Saint Paul's, which is more surprising not only because of its source but for its greater enthusiasm. 'I lost my heart,' says the Dean, 'to these New England towns and villages with their pretty frame houses, each standing in an unfenced grass plot, and the lovely avenues of elms on either side of the roadway. Nearly every house tries to express something; they are not soulless copies of each other, like a dreary English suburb. I can imagine no better place to live than among these miles of uncrowded, happy-looking homes. . . . Here, I said, is the best that Anglo-Saxon civilization can do, and, thank heaven, it is all as safe as anything can be in this naughty world.'

This praise speaks clear, for it is well known that Dean Inge is not 'too soon made glad,' and he, as an Englishman, knows what little towns should be like. I know of nothing written by any Englishman that has flattered my home-pride more than this paragraph, unless it be William Archer's assertion that Concord is, upon the whole, the most satisfactory place of pilgrimage for people of the Anglo-Saxon race. After reading such words we can afford to think of Mrs. Trollope and all that old unpleasantness with an indulgent smile.

Ellington is still a pleasant town, with only two thousand inhabitants in its thirty-five square miles, but Sill does less than justice to the land between it and the River. The 'worthies' of East Windsor have been three: maize, gin, and Jonathan Edwards. Of

these, only Edwards remains with us in any sense to be
tested to-day, and we are not the people to estimate
him justly; yet it ought to be clear even now that nowhere on this continent have we bred a better brain,
a tenderer heart, or a more exalted religious genius
than his. No more than Pascal could he work his common sense free from his logic but we should not fail to
see that it was a giant who struggled in the toils. If the
plains of East Windsor had never produced anything
but his mental thews and sinews, they might still be
called prolific. To-day they produce chiefly tobacco
and bill-boards.

At Broad Brook, a factory town on the western edge
of East Windsor township, I came upon the bill-boards
full tilt. They were the outposts of the twentieth century, and apprized me that I was returning to the com-
forts and conveniences of modern civilization. I do
not mean to imply that the bill-boards in Broad Brook
are any more inane than they are in ten thousand other
towns of America, but merely that, after several days
on lonely roads, where I had been able to see the landscape at all times without peering through a lattice of
silk-hose and soft-collar 'ads,' I was more incensed by
them than usual. In the cities and along the automobile highways we become inured to these fungoid
growths of ugliness, meekly accepting them as our
desert — and indeed they do provide an accurate
measure of our degradation. But a man who has been
abroad in the country for a time recollects what were

once the rights and dignity of human nature so that upon his return he sees the bill-boards freshly, with a stab of pain, as a brutally insolent invasion.

READER — You seem more excited over this than the occasion warrants.

WRITER — If you think so, I am astonished that you have read so far in this book.

READER — Please don't be insulting. You must consider that advertisers do not address themselves to people who take long walks in the country.

WRITER — No, thank God!

READER — And you must remember that they claim to do a lot of good.

WRITER — 'Claim!' They will 'claim' anything, and while 'social service' is a going slogan of course they will claim even that. I recall that when the President of the British Association of Advertising Men sailed from Southampton, not long ago, for the great congress of his fellows in Buffalo, he 'claimed,' according to the London papers, that this meeting would advance the progress of the world by five years. There was one way, to be sure, in which the convention might have made good the boast; but I judge that they did not take it, for bill-board advertising has not come to an end.

READER — I think your objections to advertising are largely sentimental. Our modern civilization could not get along without it.

WRITER — My objection to bill-boards is not so much that they smear the landscape with triviality

and garish ugliness, for those who care about that can
still get away from them. What angers me is that they
vulgarize the people who don't know enough to get
away. They are the national picture gallery. Where
the Athenians put the Parthenon we put a chewing-
gum advertisement. Where the Florentines erected
a statue by Cellini we set a picture of a girl in silk
stockings. Don't talk to me about 'our modern civilization' while we spend more to debauch the taste of
our people than we do upon educating them. We
could have bought all the best pictures in the world —
since the monetary argument is the only one likely to
'appeal' to the men who are responsible — with the
millions we have spent during the last ten years in
helping Americans to distinguish between three or four
equally contemptible cigarettes.

READER — Don't you think this chapter is about
long enough?

WRITER — The difficulty is in bringing it to an end
with an appropriate string of verses, in the heat I have
got myself into. Nothing short of another Inferno
would quite suffice. I should have a jolly time writing
one, as Dante had with his — placing the more male-
ficent advertisers in their appropriate corners of hell
and making the punishment fit the crime. I have one
of them already selected for the hole into which Judas
was crammed at the very bottom. Shall I write it? Or
would it seem too long?

READER — I think I could do without it.

WRITER — Well, then, I will tell you a story instead.

L'APRÈS–MIDI D'UN FAUNE

HE came out very timidly from the forest at the foot
of the hill, pausing a long time behind the larger pine
trees to peer across the valley with serious, wondering
eyes. He had heard tales of those who lived down here
— creatures like himself, and yet unlike; for they had
no cloven hoofs, no horns behind the ears, and they
rode storming through the woods on huge raucous
monsters of metal. He wondered what they could be
like, yet he feared nothing so much as an actual en-
counter that would answer all his questions.

But he could neither see nor hear anything at all
alarming. There were only wide quiet meadows before
him, tremulous in the heat of a September afternoon.
Half way up the opposite hill a little aspen tree twin-
kled in the breeze. A hawk was floating far overhead.
He stepped cautiously into the clearing.

Suddenly he smelt water. He turned his ear away
from the breeze and listened intently. He *heard* water!
It must be a river, or at least a large brook — a precious

thing in the hills where he had always lived and
whither his fathers had been driven long ago. Forgetting all about the hornless creatures said to infest this
region, he crossed the clearing in a flash and leapt head-
long into the stream.

After half an hour of splashing, swimming, and
floating on his back, he stepped out, dripping, and sat
for a while on a flat rock beside the bank. It was very
cool and comfortable there. He thought he would like
to stay a long time. Gauzy domes of azure and emerald came sailing down the water, and he selected the
larger ones and tried to hold his breath until they
burst. Dragon-flies went up and down like tiny boats
of the air. A sand-piper flew down near at hand and
bobbed and pirouetted until the faun laughed and
threw a stone at it.

Leaning forward with his head sunk between his
hairy shoulders, he could see his reflection in the
stream, disturbed ever so little by the ripple circling
out from the drops that fell from his fetlocks. This
was a new thing, for the streams of his country were
too swift to carry a clear image. A few feet from the
bank grew some slender reeds, good for whistles. He
thought he would get one of these and notch it into a
pipe, as an old and very learned faun had taught him
to do, and then make a tune about the happiness he
felt in sitting there among the shadows by the cool
water.

But just as he slipped down from the rock he saw a
thing that sent all thought of whistles out of his head.

He stood for a full minute gazing at it while the water swirled and chuckled about his shaggy legs. Not two hundred feet from him, on the further side of the stream, sat a wonderful creature, looking as steadily at him as he at her.

Some ancestral memory told him that this was a female of the hornless and hoofless sort, and he recalled, moreover, a tradition that the females had been kind, anciently, to fauns. At any rate, *he* was not afraid. He waded the stream in a shallow place, and then crossed two long parallel lines of metal resting upon transverse logs of wood which were supported in turn by a gravel embankment. He paid little attention to this, for his gaze was fixed upon the smiling seductive eyes that looked at him unwaveringly over a polished shoulder.

He could see by this time that she, too, had evidently been taking a bath, for her hair appeared to be wet. Clearly, however, she was not bathing in a stream. She seemed to be sitting in some whitish thing that hid from him most of her body — all of it, in fact, except her head and shoulders. Ah well, he thought, that might be one of their shy little ways, and he must be prepared for such differences. In one hand she held aloft something red and oblong — he could not tell just what.

As he drew near he noticed for the first time that she had not moved. This too was a queer trick, but he must not let her see that he had observed it. Anyhow, there was still the same reassuring smile. He allowed himself to gambol a little when some fifty feet away. He threw a somersault or two, and a cart-wheel. Her gesture did not change, so that he was obliged to decide that it was well enough suited to express surprise and admiration. He did some backward somersaults and a dazzling succession of hand-springs, with no appreciably different results.

Then he began again and went through his whole repertoire of tumbling tricks. It was a warm day, and he began to perspire. Glancing up at his audience toward the end, he saw that she held the same fixed attitude. He felt mildly disgusted.

Finally, abandoning all effort at gymnastic wooing in form, he strode straight toward her. This he knew was not according to the etiquette of fauns, but he had begun to distrust all the rules with which he was acquainted. And as he went a vague trouble dawned in his serious eyes. For the last few feet he almost ran, and when he reached her he did a curious thing — he stretched high up and laid his finger on the rosy round of her shoulder. She was hard! And she was flat! Nothing in all the lore of fauns had prepared him for this. He ran round to see how she looked on the other side. She *had* no other side!

After a second or two of reeling bewilderment the faun turned and ran very swiftly back toward the stream, toward his own hill country of horns and hoofs and females of three dimensions. The more he ran the more frightened he grew, and his blood pounded in his ears. Perhaps that is why he did not hear the scream of the lightning express as it rounded the bend. Even if he had heard it, he would only have run the faster, for he would have thought it the voice of the hard flat female pursuing him one-sidedly down the hill.

On the next morning there was something in the newspapers about a 'nude body, crushed beyond recognition, evidently that of a foreigner.' But the bathing lorelei sent across the river the same steady amorous gaze that had lured that foreigner to his death, holding aloft in her left hand a cake of reddish soap. Beneath her bathtub, in two-foot letters, ran the legend:

DO NOT MERELY BATHE

USE JENKINS'S KLEENZIT

IT FLOATS!

IX

ALL THE VALES AND HILLS AMONG

What more felicitie can fall to creature
Then to enjoy delight with libertie,
And to be Lord of all the workes of Naiure,
To raine in th' aire from th' earth to highest skie,
To feed on flowres and weeds of glorious feature,
To take whatever thing doth please the eie?

— SPENSER

To read the Book of Nature, a man must walk over the leaves.
— PARACELSUS

FOR the fifty miles or so inter-vening between Windsor and Salisbury I must refer the reader to the map and gazetteer of Connecticut, reminding him again that this is not a book of reference. About all this region I could write interminably with a galloping pen, if it were not for the hampering convention, brought about by collusion between publishers and readers, that every book shall have an end. As matters stand, I must leave it to be imagined how my walking-stick and I plodded through the sandy pine-flats of the Granbys, how we toiled up North Canton Hill and got lost there among the tangled woods, how we tapped our way through the wilds of Barkhamsted, how we wandered

and loafed and slept in Winchester, and how we pulled
our vagabond selves together when we came into Norfolk where rich men go to play golf in summer and
poor men go to paint.   And the reader is to know that
all this land west of the River is different from the
lands to the eastward, that it is wilder and takes on
more and more the look of a frontier country as you go
up into it.   Fewer ghosts are met there because there
have been fewer people to die.   The reader is to know
also that while I climbed higher into the hills the summer vanished and autumn came, with frosty nights,
banners of gold in the hickories, and the beginning
rustle of fallen leaves.   And finally he should know
that across all the miles that stretch from the River
clear to the western boundary I sang, while my stick
kept time, the best of all walking songs, to a tune that
I had made for it — a song that puts a heart of valor
beneath the ribs of famine and makes mole-hills out of
mountains.   Of course I mean the walking-song of
Autolycus:

> Jog on, jog on, the foot-path way,
> And merrily hent the stile-a;
> A merry heart goes all the day,
> Your sad tires in a mile-a.

This was not by a good deal the only song I had with
me, for I carried all the way, in knapsack or pocket, a
little green volume of verse that has been my companion upon many a similar ramble.   I can scarcely
see it standing on my shelves without thinking of the
days we have spent together, for I have carried it hun-

dreds of miles, among mountains, beside great rivers, along and across the sea. It reminds me of a gray boulder in the middle of a mountain stream in California where I have sat beneath the alders through many afternoons, now reading a page and then looking down the dancing water. It brings before me that noble grove of beeches on Saint Catherine's Hill that looks down on the English Winchester, where a few people go every year to think about John Keats. Its pages are stained by the pine needles of Montana, by the maple-keys of Wisconsin, by the daisies of England, and by the dust of Connecticut goldenrod. They are darkened here and there by the water of the Concord River, into which the book once fell with me out of a canoe. The binding is not quite what it was after a certain grievous experience with barbed wire in New Hampshire. The fly-leaves are pencilled full of memoranda about how to get from place to place in Nova Scotia, what trout-flies to use in the Dartmouth Land Grant, and what supplies to lay in at the next village grocery. But considering that the book is all made up of poems about 'the wide blue air and the emerald cup of the sea,' I like it all the better because it so obviously knows something at first hand about the wilds of which it sings.

And then too, of course, I had a walking-stick. Indeed, when I think how friendly this companion was on every mile of my ramble, I am sorry for having said, a good way back, that I took the trip alone. For if the stick did not actually originate any ideas of its own, at least it punctuated and enforced and otherwise embellished a good many of mine — and what more than that can be asked of a companion?

Let it be clearly understood that I am talking about a walking-stick, and not about a cane. The differences between the two may not be immediately discernible to the unpracticed eye, but they are nevertheless deep and fundamental. Generally speaking, the cane is recognizable by its glossy smoothness, and by its handle of gold or silver or ivory, whereas the stick goes in rather for serviceability than for any gauds of outward appearance. There is a look of honesty about all genuine sticks seldom to be observed in canes. It should be remembered that the two things have come down to us along utterly different lines of descent and that they have always kept very different company. The cane is a lineal descendant of the scepter, the baton, the sword, the rapier, and it bears even to-day the sinister marks of that ancestry. But the forbears of the walking-stick are the countryman's cudgel, the single-stick, the leaping-pole, the pilgrim's staff, and the shepherd's crook. Its aristocracy, that is to say, is intrinsic and real — not based, like the cane's, upon mere public opinion. Instead of having deteriorated from a long line of slaughterous side-arms and futile badges of office, it is to-day what it has always been: a third leg, a longer arm, a weapon fit for an honest man's use, and a friend. Let the cane vaunt itself as it may, the walking-stick's ancestry is far more ancient. Scipio Africanus was named after it; Socrates always carried it; Abraham the Patriarch never stirred abroad without one. No, the cane, by comparison, is a mere upstart.

If any one thinks that I have exaggerated these differences, let him try to make friends with a cane and see what comes of it. The thing simply cannot be done. Ages of snobbery have made it about as affable as a snake. I like the stick, as I like the man, that does not hint at social distinctions and that rouses no thought of such distinctions in me. So that it be good honest wood and fits easily into my hand, I do not care at all how much it cost or what tree it was cut from. True aristocracy I think I value as much as any one, and that is precisely the reason why I dislike to see my countrymen sneer at walking-sticks as though they were canes. Why must we always pour out the baby with the bath? But perhaps if I could succeed in making the differences quite clear to them all, I should not accomplish much, for I sometimes fear that they hate real aristocracy, that is to say all genuine and intrinsic excellence, as much as they do its specious imitation.

Having broached the dangerous topic of aristocracy, I must not allow my natural modesty to prevent me from pointing out that all men may be classed under the two headings of those who carry walking-sticks and those who do not. At the mere waving of this magic wand, what a swift parting of sheep from goats! On the one hand are ranged the cane-wearers all and sundry, together with the golfers, the tennis players, the people who 'take exercise' and 'keep fit,' the stern struggers, the typical business men, the four hundred, the social servants, the pillars of society, and in general the people who always know where they are going and so carry off all the tangible prizes of worldly success. On the other side appear all the saunterers and idlers in the land, the rogues and vagabonds, the tramps, the hoboes, the ne'er-do-wells, some college professors, many poets, and all essayists. This company is by far the smaller of the two, but in estimating its comparative strength one has to remember that every man in it is an individual, standing on his own legs and doing his own thinking, however faulty that may be. Each of them counts as one. If I may stand aside from this little group for the moment, I should like to say that it contains not a few minor heroes; for it takes a sort of courage to carry a walking-stick in these days and endure cheerfully the superior smiles of those who do not, to walk while all the world is riding, to live while others are earning a livelihood, to fail year after year with a happy insouciant grace while all one's fellows are careering toward a loud and garish success. It is not so much that your gentleman of the walking-stick is lazy, or even indifferent, as that some Providence or Fate is constantly reminding him where he should lay up his treasure. And the only consolation he has is that, being one of the meek, he almost literally inherits the earth. Perhaps that is consolation enough. He enjoys every mile of the way too much to think of any sort of applause at the end of it. Just because he has not set out toward any particular goal, he is surprised and charmed by almost everything he comes to in his aimless wanderings. Such is the wisdom of the walking-stick.

A walker would have been ashamed of the loitering pace I kept from the River westward, seldom making more than two miles an hour, leaning on every convenient pasture gate to gaze at cattle, writing in my

notebook, lying under trees to watch the clouds, often merely sitting on a stone by the roadside staring at asters and absorbing sunshine. The country I was walking through was quite as good, I knew, as any that lay beyond.

Some historian of the thirtieth century may divide the past into four epochs, according to the distances commonly made in a single day's journey. He will set down first the thirty-mile period, immense in duration — the age of pedestrians. Next will come the hundred-mile era of stage-coaches and bicycles, and then the reign of automobiles, establishing a scale of three hundred miles. Finally he will record the age of aërial travel, his own, in which three thousand miles may be an easy jaunt between breakfast and dinner.

But I hope that this future historian will make it clear that the men of his day have paid dearly for their speed. They will have lost the joys of the road — lilt of bird-song in the hedge, grind of gravel under foot, the smell of rick and farmyard, the biting taste of water-cress, and quiet talk at noon or twilight beneath the wayfaring tree — and will have found in their stead only distant bird's-eye views. Considering that men have been walkers rather than riders during ninety-nine per cent of their history, he will see that the love of these minutiæ of the wayside must have sunk deep in their hearts. The rambler's delight and study is in little things. He likes to make fine distinctions, comparing this hillside with that, preferring a certain beech to another, deciding after much deliberation that one old stone wall of his acquaintance is probably the best of its kind. But the man who makes three hundred miles a day does well to distinguish between one county and another, and we can imagine the three-thousand-miler peering down from the clouds through his binoculars and striving vainly to make out whether he is passing over Connecticut or Massachusetts.

One afternoon I sat for an hour on a hillside in Norfolk township and wrote this record:

The wind, which has blown steadily out of the northwest for the last two days, scouring all the caves of the sky and brightening every tinge of the autumnal maples, has given up its rush and roar. It still comes marching down the slopes of the Berkshires across the valley, but by the time it reaches the sloping pasture where I sit and listen it is content to dance, to play a little, and then to pause. The thunder of its recent storming through the woods, which yesterday crushed out of recognition all the separate languages of the trees, sweeping them into a wild confusion of leafy tongues, is over now. I begin to sort and distinguish the various voices that come to me.

Thomas Hardy somewhere says that men who spend their lives in the open are often able to distinguish the commoner trees in complete darkness by the sounds of their leaves and boughs. Much would depend, of course, upon the season of the year, and also upon the force and direction of the wind, for every tree has a wide range both of gamut and timbre. I find, however, that I can easily distinguish the deep bass tone of the pine grove behind me from the whistle of the beeches in front, and I think I could hardly mistake a pine tree at midnight. The wind is imprisoned and embayed among its multitudinous thickset needles, and issues from them in a sound always likened to that of ocean surf. In the beech, however, it clashes and rasps its way across flat, hard, almost metallic surfaces. The beech is like a beautiful woman with an unpleasant voice.

Now and then I catch a third kind of arboreal music from the grove of oaks two hundred feet down the hill, but this is too remote to particularize. Near at

hand, the oak would give me little trouble in the darkest night, at any rate if its leaves were sere, for the
flapping of old oak leaves against the twigs is the dry-
est sound in nature. And
certainly it would be
quite easy to name the
poplar blindfolded, if
only there were leaves
enough to keep up the
perpetual chattering and
fairy hand-clapping that
seems to come from the
tree itself, independent
of any breeze.

There is something
mildly surprising about
this experience — sitting
here on this open hillside
to give the ear its innings, escaping for a while from
the tyranny of the eye, remembering once more that
the landscape has not only a face but a voice, many
voices. It is as though a door were suddenly opened
that has been closed too long. For days, of course, I
have heard all this babbling, lisping, rustling, and
shouting of the trees, but not clearly because not
with full concentration. Now I suddenly realize that
I am listening to the oldest music of all, to the earliest
harps and drums and zitherns. These singers of the
forest were the progenitors of Brahms and Beethoven,
and the best of our music still remembers its noble

ancestry.   I remember how, according to Mommsen, the Romans used their most gifted flute-players and

musical priests to interpret the oracular singing of the groves, and I remember the sacred oak of Dodona to whose rustlings men listened devoutly, as to the voice of God, for hundreds of years. I begin to understand that most ancient and most graceful of superstitions — tree-worship.

Next in importance to the music of leaves is that of the insect orchestra, and in this too I find a surprising variety.   On this single hillside there are innumerable fiddlers and fifers and tiny tympani playing all together in a most harmonious ensemble. I cannot name half of the instruments. Beneath the insistent chant of crickets and the dry whirr of grasshopper wings there is a medley of anonymous cheepers and chirpers that defies my entomology. My ignorance is most ungrateful, for although these voices compose only the underbrush of the day's music, I should miss them greatly if they were suddenly stilled. I am glad to think that they were appreciated by the Greeks, that the Japanese love them still, and that they have had something like justice done them by one American poet, Madison Cawein.

At this season of the year there is little bird-song to be heard, and to-day even the calls are infrequent. The scream of the jay, delightful to me for some obscure reason in spite of its harshness, is heard now and then. Chickadees are saying their own names over and over in the pine grove, changing now and then to the whistled minor interval they have taken from the phœbe and improved upon, and sometimes they are answered by the laconic nuthatch who hunts in their company. A hearty good-natured fellow the nuthatch is, and although he is somewhat pot-bellied and a gross feeder one cannot help liking him. All his character is in his voice, which seems to bubble up like Falstaff's through layers of fat. Here, as on the ridge above Fairford, the bluebirds and robins are convening for their long flight, and their restless chirping notes express in the same breath both reluctance and eagerness to be gone. Far up above me a crow is cawing as he flaps heavily over, with the whole dome of the sky for his sounding-board. On the dry bough of some distant tree a woodpecker is drumming, not interrupting but seeming to deepen and intensify the stillness of the woods.

Under the songs of leaves, insects, and birds there lives another sound, far more tenuous and ethereal, to which a trained, intensely listening ear can sometimes pierce. This is that

> Little noiseless noise among the leaves
> Born of the very sigh that silence heaves

that John Keats heard and that Dorothy Wordsworth

described in her Journal, twenty-five years earlier, as 'that noiseless noise which lives in summer air.' As usual when there is a comparison, Dorothy is more nearly right, for the sound seems, at least, to have no connection with leaves or with any other substantial thing; it seems really to live an independent life, and in the air. Chateaubriand also associated the sound with leaves, as Keats did, or at least with '*la cime indéterminée des forêts*' — a magical phrase! In a famous passage of his 'Atala' he speaks of it: '*Aucun bruit ne se faisait entendre, hors je ne sais quelle harmonie lointaine qui régnait dans la profondeur des bois; on eût dit que l'âme de la solitude soupirait dans toute l'étendue du désert.*' All the words that I can find to name this sound by seem to do it violence, for it is neither a hum nor a whisper, neither a babble nor a susurration, but something fainter and finer than any of these; and so perhaps it is as well to fall back upon Chateaubriand and to call it '*je ne sais quelle harmonie lointaine.*'

And under even this is there not still another sound, yet more ethereal? I cannot be quite certain, but once or twice I have been almost sure that I heard it — on rocky mountain tops far above the noise of leaves or of falling water, above the eagle's scream. What I am sure of is that perfect silence does not exist on this side of the grave, and that the gradations of quietness must therefore be more numerous than we suppose. If my hearing were sufficiently acute it may be that I could strip off like so many husks all the sounds of leaves, insects, and water, all the calls of men and ani-

mals and birds, the rumor of the breeze in my ear and
the faintly beating drum of my heart, and finally even
this mysterious *harmonie lointaine* itself, until I should
get down at last to the sound of the earth's breathing
and the low song it hums as it goes swinging on its
way.

Far down in the valley some one is shingling a house,
and in certain freaks of the wind the strokes of his
hammer reach me still distinct and clear. This too is a
sound of Nature's, no less than the hammering of the
woodpecker. The sky makes every hammer-stroke instantly its own. I hear the report of a gun in the woods
to westward, and the echoes dart back and forth across
the valley like voices of the taciturn hills. And now
the whistle of a locomotive winding below along the
Housatonic floats dreamily up to me. Even that sound
is at home here, and strangely beautiful. Five miles of
wood and dell have worn away all its harshness. Millions of leaves have sifted and strained and refined the
scream of the steel whistle until, by the time it reaches
my ear, it seems as indigenous as the call of the bluebird in yonder thicket. It suggests to me none but
quiet thoughts, and deepens 'the sleep which is among
the ancient hills.'

Noblest of all sounds to be heard in the country is
the speech of the steeple, for this, more than any other,
'humanizes the landscape and makes us feel that the
little earth is really our home. America, of course, is
comparatively poor in bell-music, yet I heard it that

same evening as I walked toward Norfolk through the twilight. It was the voice of humanity singing in antiphon with the fading colors of the sunset, deepening their beauty, saddening and sacring all the air. And I remembered how I had heard this same music of the sky two years before, on an English hill. I remembered how quiet the evening was about the lofty clump of beeches where I stood, and that even the field of

barley sloping down into the shadows was unstirred by
the faintest breeze. Sprinkled along the crooked lanes
below me were a score of villages with not a voice to
betray them. The last lark was coming down from the
sky, his wings quivering against the embers of sunset in
a final ecstasy of farewell. The dark fields, the darkening hill, the trees on the hill where some faint light
still shone, were one great audience, hushed and expectant. And then a vast voice far below began to
utter majestic speech. It said all that I had wanted to
say about the beauty of that time and place, and then
went on to a hundred deeper things. It sang the sorrow
of earth and our fear of the darkness that islands our
little light, but also it sang our heroism in the face of
everlasting defeat. It was man's voice talking to the
stars. Oh, a noble bell! I hope that in a thousand
years New England may have such another.

And I remembered also, as I walked into Norfolk,
the summer evening years before when I climbed the
bell-tower of a cathedral city in the south of England
and rang the curfew. Except for the verger standing
by, there was no one with me up there among the
shadows, yet I felt all the excitement and the eagerness
to live up to a great occasion that an orator may have
just before addressing a vast audience. For there,
through that huge bronze five-hundred-year-old throat
'swinging slow with sullen roar' above me, I spoke to
half a county in a tongue that it knew far better than I.
Amberley heard me far to eastward, and little Didling
hidden among the downs to the north. The Arun

heard a familiar voice, although perhaps in no familiar accents — and proud should I be to think that it did not stammer. My call rang clear to Selsey Bill and to the fishing boats off Bagnor. It made the evening holy

for many a countryman plodding homeward through the twilight behind his cart, and for many a wandering man who would sleep out among the hills that night beneath the stars. I thought of all these things, I remember, although the sinuous twitchings and writhings of a rope stirred suddenly into life beneath a thousand-

pound bell are quite enough to keep a tyro fully occupied. One does not address the South Downs of
England in a language they have had by heart since
William the Conqueror without a sense of responsi-
bility. That was a proud moment.

England has long been known as 'The Ringing Isle,'
and Connecticut will not soon overtake her; but every
advance we make in the founding and ringing of bells
will be a step toward truer patriotism and deeper love of
home. For the village speaks most persuasively through
its steeple, and just as we do not know a man by his
face and manner only but wait to hear his voice, so we
cannot be sure about a town until we have heard its
bell. If it has none, how can it even know itself? And
certainly we should learn to put the speech of the
steeple to something besides dull or utilitarian uses. It
will do something to sanctify trivial or even base em-
ployments, but we defraud ourselves by using it in
these alone. It is the simplest and most majestic
language we have found for the phrasing of thoughts
and emotions almost unutterable, this language of
metal tongues and deep bronze throats spoken from
platforms of stone. It sings for us all that we have
found to say in answer to the songs of the earth and of
the sky.

THE BELL

FAINTLY, far away,
When the dusk comes down,
    when the dew falls,
Sounds an aërial voice
Under the few first stars. . . .

One after one, in the pool
Of quietness, tone after tone drops,
Wakening circles that wash
The shores of a hundred hills.

Mile after mile through the leaves
Of the shadowy listening tree-tops
Travels that alien voice,
That vast slow-syllabled speech,

Hinting at meanings beyond
The last dim guess of the pine tree,
Fabling a sorrow too old
For the ancientest hill to have known.

Ah, sad deep voice of Man,
Heart-broken, courageous, and lonely,
Giving the distance a tongue,
Dowering the dusk with a soul!

X
THE MOUNTAIN

I have seen everything except the wind.
— JOHN KEATS

THE king of all winds that blow over Connecticut is the Great Northwest, and Salisbury is where he comes from. He has his cave somewhere among the ravines of Mount Riga, or else on the slopes of Bear Mountain that look down upon three states. When he is abroad and in his glory no man can think of anything for very long, or read a book, or even write notes for such a book as this. He finds it impossible to sit still. He must walk . . . and walk south-eastward.

Looking out from my eastern window in Salisbury one morning, I could see that the Northwest Wind had marked the day as his own. Outlines of distant hills were chiseled clear against the colors of sunrise, and the sky was filled with a hurry of vivid unraveling vapors. Every bough and twig of every tree was straining in the wind — tossing, sinking, blown sidewise, buffeted and shaken — and among the aster and chicory flowers below my window the early-fallen leaves were whirling. It was such a day as only the king of winds can make,

a day brilliant and metallic, almost dazzling, flashing
with colors reflected from a billion polished surfaces,
with colors revived and blown bright, with colors fallen
from the day-spring. After a week of desultory lounging through the landscape, I felt that here was a
walker's day made to order. I heard the Red Gods
calling.

On the high ridge traversed by the Indian Mountain
Road I found the Northwest Wind at home. He was

blowing the world clean of
yesterday and making all
things new as they were on
creation's morning. Down
went the dim, the dull, the
gray, before his onset, scurrying off into obscure corners;
up went the green, the gold,
the blue, and all brave colors that prosper in stainless
weather. Streams and ponds changed from olive to
amethyst. Across the ever-deepening sky endless
fleets of cloud drove past. The grass and weeds and
flowers of the wayside, the stoutest trees, and even the
hills, seemed to be tugging at their anchors. The wind
was cleansing the globe, making it ready to shine
among the glories of sunset like an opal held high up
where the tides of light would wash through and
through.

Every bird that leaped from ground or twig was

obliged to join, willy-nilly, in the procession, for whatever may have been his original intention, he found
himself, upon alighting, at some distance, greater or
less, to the east of where he set out. Even the inde-
fatigable slow-flapping crow decided that he really preferred to go eastward after all. In the early morning
many birds seemed to think that there must be some as
yet undiscovered trick of tacking that would enable
them to fly, if not in the eye of the wind, at least at such
an angle as to hold their own; but in the afternoon most
of them had given up this notion and were flying before
the gale. Even this was not easy for all of them. Mead-
ow-larks were tumbled about most ludicrously. The
goldfinch, of course, had discovered long before that
the wind is like a sea of tossing billows, and he went
bounding easily over the crests and into the troughs,
audibly counting off each wave as he flew. The robin,
always a dashing and reckless flier, was caught again
and again in these waves of wind and drenched with
their spray. A sudden gust would lunge at him and
twist his tail, and down he would come, turning half a
somersault as he struck the ground. Instantly, however, after righting himself, he became a deeply pre-
occupied bird, looking as dignified as was to be expected considering that his neck and tail feathers were
constantly ruffled and blown askew. Having recovered
his equanimity he would take the wing again — eastward. I wondered whether several weeks of wind from
the northwest would not bank up all the bird-song of
America against the Atlantic coast.

The Northwester is an impressive athlete. See his dealings with the trees. Watch his buffets and his feints, his twists and tweaks, his jiu-jitsu and catch-as-catch-can wrestling. Watch him race the cloud-shadow up the hill, trampling the grasses with invisible feet. Nothing could elude that speed if he could only keep it up. Reaching the summit, however, and the old wood that roots there, he forgets the race and becomes a musician. All day he has been calling and shouting. Now he sings. But expect no gentle piping on oaten reeds from him, for he has only a burly battering note, a masculine music. The forest boughs are his harp, and he beats them with iron fists. Deeper in the wood he pours a more thoughtful harmony among the interlacing branches, but soon, on the other side, you hear the skirl of pipes and the roll of multiple drums. No more than Rubenstein in a frenzy of improvisation does he care for the few false notes he scatters among the millions. He carries the heights of song by storm. . . . And now he has come to the edge of the wood, sobered a little by the tangled shadows, confused by the clashing boughs. Again the great blue vault, his playroom, stretches over. Again the tall grasses waiting for his feet. Again a cloud-shadow ready for a race. After it, down the hill, through the meadow, goes he with swift invisible feet, an athlete once more.

Of all the towns in Connecticut that I know Sharon is the most beautiful, with the serene self-confident beauty of a woman who has made loveliness her profession. Little Gilead has more of the wilding tang, and Fairford is a blowsy devil-may-care hoyden always putting her worst foot foremost yet somehow ensnaring the heart, and then of course there is Middle Haddam to remind me that comparisons of this sort are always as unjust as they are unprofitable. But Sharon, at any rate, is a very fine town, full of majestic elms and stately houses, seated on a lofty hill and looking out north and west over many a mile of blue hill country. To live in Sharon should be a liberal education. There must have been some civilized people there from the very beginning, to lay out its lordly avenue along the ridge, to plant its quadruple row of elms, to build its houses, many of which have the delicate distinction of the eighteenth century, and then to preserve all this for the slow ripening of the years. As I ate my luncheon beneath a secular elm at the end of the avenue, I thought very respectfully of the people of Sharon, early and late, for I saw that they had mastered what I must call, for lack of a better name, the Art of the Village. This is a very exigent art indeed, producing an unforeseen beauty by a sort of communal composition as the outward mark of whatever beauty and dignity there may be in the people themselves. Money alone will not do the work; it only serves to emphasize the essential depravity of those who think it will. There is no drearier sight than the town that has been built with money unmixed with intelligent affection, unless it be the once beautiful town that money has captured and killed. In Sharon, I judge, there has always been money enough, but other things of greater importance have been at work there also. There have been imagination, refinement, and love of place. There has been a strongly concentrated patriotism. Although no individual in the early years ever saw in his mind's eye the completed village as a painter must see his finished picture, many individuals have worked together toward a better end than any one could have imagined. In the Art of the Village Sharon is one of America's masterpieces.

The road over Skiff Mountain from Sharon to Kent is some thirteen miles in length. On that road I saw perhaps ten houses, and half of these were deserted; for I was coming once more into a region of ghosts. Here again were the old stone walls running through unbroken woodland, and here were apple orchards recaptured by the forest. No better apples are to be had anywhere than the one I picked up in a dense thicket near the top of the mountain. Ages of culture went to the making of that apple, yet there was no sight or sound of human habitation anywhere about — nothing but a brambly wilderness. But going on two hundred yards I saw in the brush beside the way first a ruined chimney and then a worn door-step, with the inevitable lilac bush. They told the story.

It is strange to think as one walks among these untenanted townships that the men who once lived here were an unusually begettive race. Any adjacent graveyard will show that. For the women of Connecticut a century ago child-bearing was a steady occupation, pursued year in and year out, which might well have been classed among the dangerous trades. Hard as the life of the farmer usually was, the graveyard record shows that he frequently outlived three wives. One sees how the economic conditions of the time and place worked together with the Biblical injunction so as to make a virtue of the philoprogenitive instinct, for children provided the cheapest form of labor. But something like a hundred years ago this haste of the New England Puritans to replenish the earth began to show signs of abatement, and the few that are left have

scarcely any children whatever. Of the three last-surviving descendants of Keep-the-Good-Faith Sawyer, John went west and was never again heard from, Sarah died an old maid, and Jake went on the town. To-day you can find only a gaping cellar-hole, a dying lilac bush, several miles of good stone wall, and perhaps one sound apple to mark the scene of the family's long heroic toil.

This part of New England reminds me of the gigantic chestnut cadavers that still hold up their mighty arms

here and there in Connecticut, rigid in death, remnants
of the host that once peopled all the land. Scions spring
every year from their roots, but die before they mature.
Yet there is life in these dead trunks even now; they
are excellent cradles for woodpecker eggs. Just so there
is life in the dead trunk of Connecticut, though it is of a
sort that would astonish the founders. The millionaire,
the Pole, and the Jew make no more complaint of
Connecticut than the woodpecker does of the chestnut.
They do not feel that it is old and moribund, but find it
quite to their mind. They see no ghosts.

My road was often no more than a cart-track through
the woods, and it was printed thickly with hoof-marks
of deer. Partridges caromed away with a startling
rattle of wings. Once I caught a glimpse of a fox sitting
on his haunches in a little clearing twenty paces from
the road and staring straight into my eyes. As the
afternoon wore away the wind fell and the sky was
filled with clouds. The silence of the woods, after a day
of stentorian wind-song, deepened my sense of the
mystery through which I was walking — a sense that I
can express only by saying that I felt suddenly out of
tune with the place, as though I were intruding upon a
scene not meant for me, or for any human witness. It
was as though the trees were making some secret preparations, and waited for me to get by. There swept
over me a vague feeling that I was being watched by
many things at once, from above and below and from
all sides. This feeling grew and grew until all the air

seemed alive with hostility and menace. And then I came to Desolate Swamp.

The name is my own, for I could not find the place on my map, but it is the source, I think, of Macedonia

Brook. I shall remember it always as a perfect symbol of desolation. There were thirty acres of slate-gray water under a slate-gray sky, and in the water two or three hundred drowned trees, some submerged to the knees and others to the armpits, all livid in death. I thought the place was like something Dante had imagined for his *Inferno* but had left out as too terrible for words. Poe's demon had cursed it with silence, and another demon had cursed it with a blank despair which daunted the mind and would make the stoutest beholder quail.

A wholly sentimental traveler would have tried to think Desolate Swamp quite meaningless, a mere hiatus in nature; but I had been braced by twenty miles of rather hard going over the hills since morning, and so I dared to stand and face the swamp for a few minutes, wondering what it meant. And this is a part of what it said to me — although there are no words to express a message by its essence devoid of human significance:

'Soft and dreamy seeker of pleasant emotions, know that you see no farther into the realities of what you call your "Mother Nature" than a painted butterfly does in flapping from flower to flower. You too are convinced that the sun shines to warm your wings, and that the meadows are strewn with flowers to flatter your delight in color. The fear that clutches now at your heart is only the fear lest your self-love, your notion of your own importance, may have less warrant than you and your fellows have dreamed. As you stare into my vacant eyes, older than thought, older than mind-stuff, you are learning faster than ever you have in reading the wisest books. Your braggart poets have not told you such things as I tell. They say that "Nature is ancillary to Man." On the man-handled meadows of Concord, perhaps, but not on Skiff Mountain, where I still remember the dinosaur's wallowing and the scream of the sabre-tooth. They have said that "Nature never did betray the heart that loved her." Ask the ghost of Hendrik Hudson. Ask the spirits of the young men lost on Mount Everest. Ask the woman dying in childbirth. Peer down into the savageries of the under-sea. Think your way out into the infinite of the sky until the brain staggers, or down into the answering infinite of the atom. Or, merely stand and look at me. As I am now, so was the planet for innumerable ages before man came, and so it will be for endless ages after he is gone. . . . Now you may pass on — for I think you will not forget.'

No, I shall not soon forget. I had been forced to con the same lesson more than once before. Walking all day in the rain on Exmoor I had read it, and again on the rocky spine of Catalina Island, and once again on a bare mountain slope in Montana. Whenever a man steps a little aside from the thoroughfares of our steam-heated and parlor-cared modernity he is likely to find some such dreary page set down for his perusal, and he must deal with it according to whatever philosophy there is in him. Desolate Swamp set all my philosophy at defiance, for it did not pretend to be wise but only final. It made sport of all the heroism I had, for even a man who can face death cannot face the thought that life and death alike are utterly meaningless. It set me for two or three shuddering minutes outside the little circle of the Things We Take for Granted, and I saw how that circle really looks. Once more, for the third or fourth time in my life, I felt the Terror of Solitude.

But it was amusing to observe how my mind began at once to edge away from its lesson. Apparently I was a good deal like the man in Boswell who tried hard for years to be a philosopher, 'but cheerfulness was always breaking in.' It is natural enough, I said, that there should be some places not yet made ready for man's coming, and we do wrong to stare obtrusively at the vast digestive processes, like that still going forward in Desolate Swamp, by which the planet was prepared for our culminating advent. And then I thought of what a snug and habitable little globe we have made it, after all. I thought of the fires we have kindled here and there — building them on the edges of the abyss, no doubt, and lighting up only our own faces against the ring of darkness, but still . . . fires. I remembered the songs we have made to sing there about the fire, the brave high-hearted songs, as though the darkness were not. And I recalled the pictures we have painted, the music of Mozart, the spire of Salisbury, and some of our pathetic faiths and hopes and illusions.

'Oh well,' I said, 'we have not done so badly, all things considered. It may be that Nature did not foresee us; but if so we have made her open her eyes! She has brought forth no other such pathetic and marvelous thing in all her kingdoms as this heart of man, so trivial and heroic, so dauntless though so filled with fears, that smiles into the eyes of Death.'

Then I thought of my dinner, six miles away, for the sun was setting behind the Catskills. I made the air whistle with a twirl of my stick, twitched my knapsack into position, and set up the rollicking road-song of Autolycus: 'Jog on, jog on, the foot-path way.'

After leaving Desolate Swamp I passed not a single house, or none that I could see through the gathering darkness, all the way to Kent. For most of that way I burrowed downward through a tunnel of gloom, like a mole, stumbling from rock to rock and feeling the path with my stick, certain only that the water-shed I was descending would take me sooner or later to the Housatonic and so eventually to one of the river towns. An hour or more of this unsatisfactory travel by touch and hearing brought me to the welcome sound of river water, and then there were two miles of valley road still to go. A breeze awoke in the sky and blew bare the new moon, with a planet or two, over Spooner Hill, and by this pale illumination I saw in due time first the buildings of Kent School, then the bridge, and finally, the village street, with the light of my inn at the far end shining.

XI
THE VALLEY

There's night and day, brother, both sweet things; sun, moon, and stars, brother, all sweet things; there's likewise a wind on the heath. Life is very sweet, brother. Who would wish to die?
— GEORGE BORROW

Nichts ist dauernd, als der Wechsel; nichts beständig, als der Tod. Jeder Schlag des Herzens schlägt uns eine Wunde, und das Leben wäre ein ewiges Verbluten, wenn nicht die Dichtkunst wäre.
— LUDWIG BÖRNE

BEFORE eight o'clock the next morning I was walking up the valley road down which I had come on the last leg of yesterday's journey. There had been a killing frost during the night, and the thermometer still hovered at the freezing point when I left the inn. Reeds and grasses along the river's brink were necklaced with delicate collars of ice which vanished under the first touch of sun. Winter had put forth just a finger to remind us of what he could do. It was enough. So unstably poised had been the glad mood with which I set forth that morning that before I had gone a mile, although the sun was shining bravely over the shoulder of an eastern hill and the river was rippling beside the way, all my thoughts were darkened. The Spirit of Desolate Swamp, which

I had eluded the evening before, overtook me there in the valley road and dogged my steps for mile after mile, throwing its chill shadow upon my mind.

I thought of the foreman in the pocket-knife factory at Lakeville with whom I had talked for half an hour the day before, and of the pride he had shown in his little garden. How would his flowers look this morning? I thought of the million asters I had seen blowing blue in the wind beside the Indian Mountain Road. They were now wilted, crumpled, dead, after the one mysterious touch that blots out beauty like a sponge. It was not so much the passing of summer as the vast universal death which this minor extinction portended that turned my thoughts toward grief, yet I felt the summer's going very poignantly. A man's feeling about death is exactly related to the wealth and worth of what death can take from him. For two weeks I had filled my eyes with the vision of earth's beauty, and now came the overpowering realization that it was all passing away, and that I could not hold back one gesture, sound, or hue. Stoics and pious people had often told me that I should not set my heart upon transient things, but I had never been, and I am not now, much impressed,

> For Oh, the very reason why
> I clasp them is because they die.

Dodge and double as he may, a man who 'loves his life to the very core and rind' can never escape for very long the thought of evanescence. This thought seemed

to identify itself with the Spirit of Desolate Swamp and to pursue me like a wolf. First I threw to the phantom the best arguments I had ever heard for immortality. They did not delay him for an instant. Then I tossed him a few quotations from Seneca and Epictetus, reminding him that only the frail creatures of the senses perish; but he knew that very well already. And then, as a last resort, I uttered a powerful charm that I found years ago in the Meditations of Guigo the Carthusian: 'Thou hast been clinging to one syllable of a great song, and art troubled when that wisest Singer proceeds in His singing. For the syllable which alone thou wast loving is withdrawn, and others succeed in order. He does not sing to thee alone, nor to thy will, but His. The syllables that follow are distasteful to thee because they drive out that one which thou wast loving evilly.'

Undoubtedly there is a wisdom in these words far beyond the reach of Seneca; for Guigo does not attempt to deny, as the Stoics always do, the beauty of the syllables over which we pause. And there is nobility, also, in his suggestion of an endless song in which the earth and all which inherit are only the fleeting notes. Yet my phantom was not exorcised even by this potent spell. Perhaps the taint of mediævalism in that last word, 'evilly,' apprised him that the whole passage was written by a man not deeply wise; for this Spirit of Desolation that follows me is very modern, and knows right well that our passionate devotion to the transient syllables of earth's beauty is not evil at all.

So I came back from the saints and philosophers to the poets, who alone have said anything worth attending to about death because they have not tried to solve its riddle — and particularly to four lines from Andrew Marvell:

But at my back I always hear
Time's wingèd chariot hurrying near;
And yonder all before us lie
Deserts of vast eternity.

'Deserts' — that seemed to me the perfect unerring word. That the Spirit of which we all partake endures forever I had no more doubt than the old Puritan poet himself, but this abstract conviction affords no stay at all when we are thinking of the things we love. Andrew Marvell, for all his rock-ribbed faith, found no strength in it when he felt that he would look in vain through vast eternity for the woman to whom his poem is addressed. The woman herself was what he loved — the scent of her hair, the strong soft clinging of her hands, the wise and witty words she spoke — and not any chill immortality. Without her, and without the other things he had lived for, such as gardens and music and children and the Latin poets, the vast eternity which he never doubted would be really a desert. Take these away, and life lost its meaning. The thought of an eternity without them was a torture to the mind.

I tried to be very precise and definite with myself, and I said: 'If I should know that in the Hereafter all that I have cared for here would be given back to me with the single exception of the sonatas of Beethoven, my hope for that future would be lessened by just so much, and my devotion to this earth, where for a little while yet I may still hear that music whenever I wish, would be by so much increased. But I am told, on what is considered good authority, that I must give up not only this music but all the music I have ever known — everything, in fact, that makes me care for life. I am told that eye hath not seen, ear hath not heard, neither hath it entered into the heart of man to conceive, the things that are prepared for us. Well then, I can only say that these things cannot possibly interest us emotionally, and that eternity is indeed, so far as human hearts are concerned, a desert.'

Thus all my defenses were beaten down, so that I stood helpless before the onset of despair, and saw myself a dying man walking among dying trees through a world as surely doomed to death as the necklaces of ice about the river-reeds. 'Very well, then,' I said. 'It is true that I am walking in the Valley of the Shadow of Death, and that very soon I shall lie down there, never to rise, and that every flower and face and thought I have known, together with all that my fellows have thought and dreamed and made, will lie there very soon beside me. But yet . . . but yet it is a most beautiful Valley. I have always loved it, and I love it more deeply at every step that brings me nearer the end. It has become the very House of the Lord to me. Why then should I grieve to lie here forever? The things I have loved will lie with me, and I would not evade the common doom. I do not ask for a separate destiny, or

desire an immortal life denied to asters. The oak and
the ash, which are dying too, they comfort me. . . . And,
beyond all this, something too vague for words or for
clear thought, too vague almost for intuition, suggests
that from this dying world some unimaginable life may
spring as the new year springs from the ruin of the old.
Then let me 'faintly trust the larger hope.' Is there
some hint of meaning for me in these triumphant glories
in which the old year is dying all about? For it does not
dwindle and pine into the grave, but goes down troop-
ing its colors and shouting hosannas, as though it had
some confident expectation of joy. In such company,
at least I can say that I will fear no evil!'

When I had groped my way to this conclusion, not
for the first nor probably for the last time, the phantom
fell away and the sunshine brightened slowly as though
a cloud were blowing from before the sun. For he who
says that no man can be happy unsustained by a faith
in personal immortality speaks in ignorance of the human heart. Earth's vast funeral cortège goes down the
years and over the slopes of shadow to a music only
faintly mournful and thrilling with many a glad ca-
denza; and he who watches that procession, seeing it
for what it is, feels a pathos in the whole which is not
entirely sad, and looks at all of life with a tenderness of
fellowship which others may sometimes miss. Nothing
links us closer to the world about us and to the human
past than this thought of our common doom. As I
walked on, the words of a nameless wandering scholar
who tramped beside the Danube eight hundred years

ago, struggling there with the same thoughts I was thinking, came to me like a cry across the centuries. His words, in Latin a little barbarous but delicately handled, pulsated with a passionate love of life darkened by the thought of life's swift passing. How little had changed during the years that divided us! But were we divided, really? He seemed to be walking shoulder to shoulder with me beside the Housatonic as I sang and crooned his verses:

> Heu! heu! mundi vita,
> Quare me delectas ita?
> Cum non possis mecum stare,
> Quid me cogis te amare?
> Vita mundi, res morbosa,
> Magis fragilis quam rosa,
> Cum sis tota lachrymosa,
> Cur es mihi graciosa?

Along my road in the valley the frost had worked no havoc, for the trees were heavy overhead and there must have been a breeze moving there all night long. Sumacs were aflame beside the water. Grape-vines with golden leaves and clusters of deepest purple were flung over the young cedars. Spotty sycamores sent their broad plates of copper slipping and twirling down through the quiet air. Night-mist rose slowly, like a woolen blanket of vapor, from the river surface and raveled away into the blue. Odors of grapes and of wet moss and leaves mingled with the indefinable scent of river water. Throughout the twelve miles that I walked that road I never lost the voice of the stream.

Even in Connecticut there are few better roads for a
morning walk in early autumn than this forgotten lane
running up the west bank of the Housatonic under
Skiff Mountain. On both sides of the river the hills

crowd close to the stream, so that one walks there in a
deep wrinkle of the earth and forgets all the world outside. The road itself is mossy, grass-grown, comfortable
to the foot, and fair to the eye in every rod of its course.
But I had been walking in the open country too many
days to concern myself greatly about the picturesque,
which is the special interest of people who must make
the most of a little time. Mere beauty of landscape is,
for me at least, hardly more than the rouge on Nature's
cheek, and I always try to walk until I can see through
it to something better and more substantial under-

neath. A man who has a beautiful wife does not ex-
claim forever at her beauty; by and by he learns to take
it for granted, and then he may fall in love, perhaps,
with the woman herself. More moving to me than anything that a painter could have put on canvas were the
hoof-prints of three deer that had gone down the road
only an hour or two before me — a stag, a doe, and a
fawn. I followed them in one place to the water's edge
where they had stood to drink in the early morning, and
I saw that the fawn had danced there in the clean sand,
leaving what might have been the footprints of a baby
Pan. Farther on, a woodchuck started to cross the
road before me, but when he saw my approach he
ambled down the path and waited until I came near.
This he did several times, being too lazy with morning
sunshine and too fat with over-eating to run far.
Apple trees stood at convenient intervals along the
road, reaching their boughs toward me heavily laden.
The apples were already warmed on one side by the
sunshine, and on the other they were still cold from the
night.

Four or five miles up the valley road I met a farmer
jogging down toward Kent in a light wagon. I told him
that I had seen a bad hole in the road some distance
back which might break his horse's leg unless he took
care. He asked me to go back with him to help him
mend the hole, and this I did. We rolled a large rock
from the bottom of a stream running under the culvert,
dropped it into the hole, and then filled the chinks with

smaller stones and gravel. When this operation was completed the farmer lighted his pipe and began to talk, mostly about the bears and snakes and Indians he had met. During his fifty years beside the river — he was born within a mile of where we stood — he had known several members of the Scaghticoke tribe which once owned all this region, and he said that one or

two individuals were still living not far from Kent. What he had to say about bears was not remarkable, but his knowledge of snakes was wide and impressive.

He told me about a custom still observed in the district which he called the 'rattlesnake feast.' All the able-bodied males of the country-side, it appeared, are summoned on a certain day of mid-summer to hunt for rattlesnakes in the hills, and a prize is offered for the largest bag.

'But about the feast,' said I. 'Why do they call it a rattlesnake feast?'

'Because they hunt rattlesnakes.'

'Why a feast?'

'Well, they have to have something to eat, don't they?'

'Yes; but *what* do they eat?' I persisted, determined

to know whether the *pièce de résistance* of this wild meal was or was not rattlesnake meat.

'Eat! Why, they'll eat anything after a day like that. Beefsteak, doughnuts, pie, cake, beans . . . any old thing.'

I was both relieved and disappointed.

He told me of a fight he had had some summers ago with a huge copperhead snake 'more than six feet long — or pretty near anyhow.' He met this snake in a 'mowing' whither he had gone with a fork to turn the grass, and it was coiled up loosely in the sunshine when he found it upon a large low rock in the middle of the little field. The snake tried to get back to the stone wall at the field's edge, where it would be safe, and the man tried to turn and keep it in the open. He yelled himself hoarse in calling for help, but none came. Each time the 'vermin' coiled to strike the man had to retire, for the snake was longer than his fork; but when it stretched out to run he went after it with the prongs. 'I fit him,' said he, 'for more'n an hour; and half the time he was a-runnin' away and half the time I was.' I told him that if it had been my fight I should have spent the whole hour in running away.

I could have talked with this Housatonic woodsman all day long, or at least while his tobacco lasted, with profit and pleasure. He was different from the men I had met at Fairford post-office, being in every good sense an 'uplandish' man while they were of the vale. There was much of the mountain in his speech and thought, or lack of thought. He was the mountain, talking. Instead of ranging far and wide over the concerns of the county, state, and nation as the Witenagemot had done, he beat very narrow boundaries of two or three little towns, two or three mountains, and one valley. But these he knew. His mind was packed with local lore, all very concrete and vivid. Nothing seemed to excite him; he took no sides; he merely observed that such and such things were so, and then passed on. His mind was wholly passive, acquisitive, sponge-like, so that he had almost exactly the temperament and mental habit required for the making of a scholar, as that word is now currently understood. All the patience and passivity, all the indifference to questions of relative value, all the childlike veneration of facts to be found in the typical scholar, were in him. The main difference is that the scholar of the schools usually spends his life by preference upon a subject less interesting than the field of this woodsman's concentration — the village of Kent and its environs. But this is an accidental difference, for scholars do not ask '*cui bono?*'

I do not mean to imply any disrespect for him by this comparison. After all, he could do a hundred things that your 'typical college professor' — if such a creature exists — never laid a hand to. He could build boats and sail them, he could shoe a horse and drive and ride it, he could mend roads, he could fight a copperhead snake for an hour with a fork and tell the story of the fight so as to raise the hair on one's head. He knew about traps and guns and the ways of wild animals and of fish. He knew about crops and how to raise them.

He had been selectman of his town more than once and had read a few books many times. He seldom saw a newspaper. At fifty, his long body was as taut and trim as a college athlete's ought to be but seldom is. His fingers, when we shook hands at parting, seemed to be made of steel wire. He was the manliest man I met in all my journey.

The bluebirds were all about me while I sat to eat my luncheon on a little decaying bridge over a brook  that ran down to the river. I thought they might be looking for crumbs, but I had none for them. Twice while I sat there I heard a resounding splash, as of a heavy billet of wood falling into the water, from a still reach of the river near at hand; and both times I saw just after the splash a sweep of wide wings careening toward a dead chestnut across the stream. This was the osprey plunging for fish. He takes the water not head foremost, like a good diver, but with a 'belly-flop,' depending upon his needle-like claws to secure his prey. Doubtless his method is more effective than it is graceful, for he has not the look of an under-nourished bird.

For delicacy and dispatch in diving, commend me to the little kingfisher, who always dips out his fish with the least possible fuss and feathers. Not to have seen him at work is to entertain inadequate notions of what efficiency and earnestness in the pursuit of business may be. He is the official 'go-getter' of the feathered kind. Or you may think of him as the mounted policeman of the stream, always brushed and dressed in firenew uniform, always on the beat from dawn to dark, either surveying things from a dead branch or else patrolling busily along the water. There is nothing more comical in the world of birds — unless it be a pelican — than to see him rushing up and down the river with his hair blown backward, 'drinking the wind of his own speed,' and winding his policeman's rattle furiously as though he expected to find a malefactor round every corner. What he lacks in size he makes up for in dash and pertinacity. He seems to pride himself, like the American business man, in never taking a moment off. Even when you see him sitting in what looks like a brown study on a bough over the stream, you may be sure that his thoughts are on business. Let a dorsal fin dimple the surface anywhere within a hundred yards — instantly he leaps from the bough, tears through the air, dives, beaks his fish, gulps it . . . and then repeats, *da capo.*

I have never seen it observed what a wide difference there is between different birds in the matter of leisure. Some birds seem to have no leisure whatever, and others have nothing else. The wood-thrush in the tune-

ful season must live chiefly upon his own song, for he
wastes little time in foraging after grosser sustenance;
robins allow themselves large intervals of relaxation;
even the song-sparrow, busy as he looks, has not forgotten his *dulce est desipere in loco;* but the English skylark is almost ostentatious in his contempt for all gain-
ful occupations. From three o'clock of a June morning
until ten at night he does nothing but mount and sing,
descend, catch his breath, and mount again. And he
maintains this programme not only throughout the
mating and nesting seasons but throughout the round
year, for it is the Uranian Aphrodite that he celebrates.
He does not regulate his raptures by the calendar like
the chary nightingale, refusing to utter a melodious note
after midsummer day, for the most fleeting glimpse
of sun in winter will coax him up his spiral stair to shake
aloft his tangle of silver bells. He seems to know that
one lark can take the place of many lower warblers
that have posted away to Africa, and that is why his
leisure is so strenuous; that is why he must climb so
often and shower song upon a hundred outspread
acres. He belongs among the cheerful givers whom the
Lord loveth, never tithing anise and cummin like the
blackbird but eagerly pouring forth his all . . . one
thousand times a day.

What is it that makes the breath catch and the heart
leap up whenever we hear these lofty notes of the lark?
Not any beauty, I am persuaded, in the song itself.
Listening intently, you will find this most famous of all
bird songs an endless and meaningless twitter, pierc-

ingly shrill, with no pattern of rhythm, beauty of phrase, or wealth of tone. Much must be allowed for its noble setting, which is nothing less than the whole vault of the sky, and there is something so surprising in a song that falls from a cloud that we must attend and wonder. The action, also, that goes with the song, the rhythmic up-and-down, cannot fail to astonish the dullest beholder. In this bold defiance of gravitation — for it is really a tremendous feat for the bird to pour its song abroad without a perceptible breathing interval while lifting himself perpendicularly to a great height — there is enough to arouse surprise at difficulty superbly overcome.

But there is yet more marvel than all these considerations explain in the song of the lark. He is to us no mere lofty tumbler or aerial acrobat, but a spirit. His song and flight, to us earth-creepers, signifies all but pure ethereality, all but perfect triumph of spirit over flesh. He plays harder than any other creature dares to work, and he lives upon ecstasy. Although certainly the most astonishing athlete of the sky, he has no time to eat anything. After his exhausted drop into the grass — quite burnt out forever, you would say, like a spent rocket — he gives himself just time to sip a beakful of dew and then, behold! he is up again, to sing for five minutes on the one breath of air he has been able to catch. It is impossible, you observe, that he should belong to the same order as the heron and the condor and other gross feeders that think nothing but belly-thoughts all their days. The biologists have made a

mistake, regarding only his body — if he has one —
and ignoring the soul, which is nearly all of him. He is
a little brother of the angels.

Yet I am not sure whether it is the marvelous success of the skylark or his inevitable failure that wakens

the deepest reverber-
ations in the hearts
that listen below . . .
whether the predom-
inant emotion with
which we watch and
hear him is one of
envy or of sympathy.
Shelley does not bring
his lark down from
the sky; in our imag-
ination it is singing
and soaring still; but
the real lark comes
back to earth, like Wordsworth's, and as we do. That
is what makes him a more faithful and pathetic image
than the 'ineffectual angel' could understand of the
human spirit in its perpetually alternating victory and
defeat.

For listen again as he goes up, and up, borne on an
irresistible and spontaneous effervescence of boundless
glee, singing skyward, a fountain of melody, a tiny ball
sustained on a fountain's crest, held up and wafted onward by the rising song of earth's rapture, by the universal joy of being, quivering with delight, raining

gladness, singing as though no other lark had ever sung
before, determined this time, at long last, to unpack
his hoard of happiness at heaven's gate. Almost you
expect some door of the sky to swing wide and let him
through. But no. There comes a pause — not in the
song but in the upward pilgrimage. He tarries there a
moment on the steeps of cloudland, where the seas
of light wash through and all but erase his little body
from the sky. Still he aspires, he trembles on the verge,
victory seems in sight. . . . But it is not for him. He
has looked over into a promised land which he will
never enter. All that spirit clogged by the flesh can do
he has done, and it has not been enough. He feels
in every fiber the pull of the sluggish earth, and he begins to descend by little stages, reluctantly, singing,
singing still, coming back to us baffled, like a poet who
returns from his quest of the Blue Flower with only a
few torn twigs and leaves to show the way he went, but
leaving with us an abiding sense of what that wonder
must be that not even a lark can sing.

Have we not done the same thing ourselves in our
clumsier way? Ah, how many times! He almost triumphs, momentarily, over the power of darkness and
the more terrible powers of silence that doom our highest vision to voicelessness, and we seem to triumph
with him. 'Oh, high above the home of tears, Eternal
Joy, sing on!'

The sharpest possible contrast with the English skylark is found in the American brown-creeper, for he is
not only everlastingly at work, like the kingfisher, but

he is also very dull, a harmless drudge. He uses for
work, in every moment of life, all the little strength the
moment brings, and he has no margin of time or spirits
left over for anything so wasteful as joy or song. His
feeble wings are not for aërial gambols but for business.
One simply cannot imagine him as sitting idly on a
bough like a hermit thrush and inviting his soul during
hour after hour that might be devoted to the serious
business of worm-finding. He has the ignoble wisdom
of Poor Richard's Almanac and regulates his life by
precautionary proverbs. What he needs more than
anything else for his soul's good is to get very drunk indeed on some arboreal tipple. But he never will. He
cannot spare the time. (The skylark, on the other
hand, is never sober.)

Watch the creeper as he spirals up a tree trunk. He
seems the concentrated essence of elm tree — a portion
of the elm detached by the tree for purposes of self-
examination, and still largely wooden. He has taken
only part of the step from vegetal to animal life; or perhaps it would be better to say that, having taken the
whole step he was aghast at his own temerity and went
half way back again. Compare him with the heavy-
headed exuberant nuthatch, or with the still more
vigorous woodpecker who hammers his way into a log
with the force of a miniature pile-driver and then works
off surplus enthusiasm on a tin roof. Nothing goes to
waste with the brown-creeper — not color, sound, size,
motion, or even shape. As he hangs there clamped to
the bark, the curve of his back, completed by his tiny

scimitar of a bill and by the stiff shafts of his propping
tail, makes almost a complete half-circle — just the
ideal shape for his business. He has the student-stoop,
and as he shuffles along from cranny to crevice he has
for all the world the look of a feathered pedant in some
vast library picking up footnotes.

A dull life, certainly, whether successful or not, is
this of the creeper; but who shall say that it has no
compensations? For one thing, he ought to have a
good conscience. In the dark watches of the night no
memory rises up to smite him of a tree-trunk half
examined or of any tiny crevice left unexplored. His
also should be the mild satisfactions that spring from
even the narrowest field of knowledge intensively
cultivated. His studious aspect does not belie him, for
probably no other creature on earth has a knowledge
comparable with his of certain grubs and worms. Many
a human reputation has been won by researches of
narrower range. He is entitled to be written down
Doctor of Philosophy, and to be invested with '*omnia
Jura, Honores, Dignitates, quæ ad hunc gradum per-
tinent*.' In addition to his own special field in entomology he knows one other thing thoroughly well — the
barks of certain trees. He often builds his nest in a
crevice of the bark. The bark is his bed, library, office,
and dining-table. All day long he scrambles over it
with a microscope, and when the rain falls with such
force that he has to knock off for an hour he clings to
it motionlessly, inert, dreaming barky dreams.

Conscientious he is, then, and economical, regular in

his habits, exemplary in his moral conduct, and wonderfully thorough. But I feel a certain strain in trying
to discover and report his virtues. When all is said,
he remains a hopelessly dull fellow. If I were given a
choice, I should prefer to be a skylark.

When these notes on the novel topic of leisure in
birds were finished I lay back with my head on my
knapsack, stretched out at full length on the bare
boards, and gazed at the sky through the flickering

leaves. Lassitude is one thing, and the rest well earned
by labor of body or brain is another, but far better
than either of these is what I may call the active re-
pose of a man neither sluggish nor weary, in perfect
health of mind and members, who slips the belt off the
wheel and lets the planet spin without his assistance.
We have seen and envied the power to do this in the
disappearing people of the South Seas, we have seen it
in young children, it may be found admirably described and exemplified in some pages of Walt Whitman's 'Specimen Days,' it may be what Wordsworth
meant by 'a wise passiveness'; but among what are
called 'civilized men' it is rare beyond belief. We are
all of us possessed by the grotesque notion that health,
when we have it, is never an end in itself but a means
— that it must always be used for some ulterior purpose rather than be enjoyed for its own sufficient sake.
I myself have long known as a matter of theory that
there are few commodities to be had at the world's
counter more desirable than health — by which I
mean, of course, not the mere absence of weakness or
disease but something positive, riant, and glowing, a
mood or condition in which body and mind and soul
strike the tonic triad together in perfect accord. And I
know also that whenever we pay down health even for
those very few things that may be better in themselves, they lose their luster before we have them under
our arms and march out of the shop. I have known
this for twenty years, and yet the days, the hours even,
in which I have fully lived up to my knowledge are so

few that I can now remember most of them. They have been my pinnacle days, my hours on Pisgah.

We have to strip off many grave-clothes of custom, of humdrum and routine, and of dull respectability before we can complete this resurrection, this rediscovery of the simple joy of being, reduced to being's simplest and most satisfying terms. He who thinks it can be done by mere indolence — well, let him try. The mystics have their way, the poets another, and the yogis of the East a third; but a method better suited than any of these to most modern Americans, probably, is to walk twenty or thirty miles a day for two weeks on end in the open country, lounging through the landscape with no particular goal, entertaining cheerfully whatever thoughts or fancies may fly into one's head but thinking of nothing either very deeply or very long. I like this method best of all because it takes the body along with one, whereas the Oriental *ascesis* usually tries to leave the body behind. On this whole matter no one, so far as I know, has ever said a truer word than Thoreau's: 'Do not look for inspiration unless the body is inspired too.' I like to remember that the word 'ascetic' once signified an athlete.

In the early twilight I saw again, over the crest of a hill, the elms of Sharon, and I was glad to walk once more down that lordly avenue.

'To the rapid traveler,' says Thoreau, 'the number of elms in a town is the measure of its civility.' By this good test nearly all the old and little towns of Connecticut are highly civilized, but among the best of all are Salisbury, Sharon, Canaan, and Cornwall. Although we have come to take elm trees for granted, the fact tells us more about ourselves than it does about them. Familiarity would never have bred contempt, or even indifference, if we had been worthy of such companions. To see them lift their splendid arches over an avenue where the traffic of the common day streams by is to learn a deep lesson in tolerance. When we see them at evening splintering the shafts of sunlight among their boughs and spreading splendor through the town, they seem to have some hope for us fairer than we deserve. We should think not less but more of them because they are all about us, thronging our streets and thoroughfares with witchery and brushing ten thousand farmhouse gables with their wings.

No tree that retains so much of forest freedom is more completely civilized than the elm. It reaches its greatest height and beauty in the river valleys and the pastures where men have long been dwelling. With a courtly grace devoid of hauteur it drops benefactions upon us as though it had the homes of men in a special care. Those subtle harmonies, for example, which all may see between the elms of New England and the older houses — a certain restraint and dignity in both that never passes into coldness — may not be altogether the results of a random good fortune, for men could not build wastefully or ignobly with the elms so near at hand to guide their taste and to rebuke their extravagance. And who shall say that this refining influence has not gone farther than architecture, making itself felt even in the lives of men and women?

Beauty can never be quite forgotten or ignored where elms are standing. They lead the eyes irresistibly upward by gracile delicacies of line, and our thoughts go with our eyes until they are lost in the tracery of intricate boughs, from which it is but a step to the clouds of noon or to the midnight stars. Do not suppose, therefore, that New England could have been quite the same without them. Do not think to know New England thoroughly, or even any of its important products, such as the poetry and prose of Emerson, without knowing elm trees. For you are to observe that the beauty of the elm is chiefly in its structure, best seen when the boughs are quite or nearly bare, and that this beauty is intellectual in its effect. I do not mean to disparage the midsummer elm, for its leaves add sails to the branches, enabling them to balance up and down with a grace of wafture never seen in any other tree. With leaves to lend it motion and variety of light and shadow, the elm in midsummer dress is a high-bred lady of the old magnificent time; but the month of the elm's real glory is April, when the twigs are faintly tinged with maroon flowers. This touch of color is just enough to underscore the tree's supreme beauty of form, compounded of grace and power. With an athletic spring and spread it combines great length of trunk and of tapering bough and pensile twig which sets it above even the stately eucalyptus and the European beech.

The Autocrat of the Breakfast Table once pointed out that provincialism 'has no scale of excellence in man or vegetable; it never knows a first-rate article of either kind when it has it, and is constantly taking second- and third-rate ones for nature's best.' The people of New England should no longer allow a timid provincialism to prevent them from saying that their elms are the finest trees in the world. At present, although they have been cherished by ten generations of Americans, they are still unpainted and unsung; but they are so certainly framed for classic celebration that we may be sure they will some day have the wide fame they deserve. In the meantime, such an avenue of elms as that of Sharon is itself a poem and a picture, surviving to remind us of what has been and may yet be again.

The sun had gone down when I came out at the farther end of the vista and saw before me a large Colonial house, four-chimneyed, under elm and maple trees, and on the ample lawn a man raking leaves. He raked with fervor and enthusiasm, yet not as though he enjoyed the task but with something almost vindictive in his energy. I leaned against a tree to watch him.

Leaf-raking had always seemed to me a contemplative and leisurely task, but it did not seem so to him. He hacked and slashed among the flying leaves in a sort of fury, and when I went closer he neither looked my way nor spoke. Finally, not so much because I wanted an answer as to break an awkward silence, I said an awkward thing:

'Why don't you leave them where they are?'

One does not know where such remarks come from. They seem to say themselves, bubbling up from wells of thought deeper than consciousness. No sooner were the words uttered than I realized how exasperating it is to a man hard at work for an idle onlooker to imply that all his labor is futile and might as well be left undone. Probably my question was the less welcome because the raker himself had a suspicion that his work was almost useless. A wind had arisen as the sun went down, and it twitched the leaves from his neatest piles. It gathered reënforcements and whirled the leaves helter-skelter across the grass he had just swept clear. Still more leaves were shaken down from the boughs above us. Trees and wind seemed to be in conspiracy against him, as though he were doing something out of harmony with the total scheme of things. Then I came by and ranged myself on the side of the rebellious elements. It was too much. His rake stopped in mid-swing. He set it upright on the ground, rested his hands upon it, and looked at me steadily with an expression of subdued rancor.

'Why not leave them where they are?' he quoted, with emphatic scorn. 'Because they wouldn't stay where they are for one minute. They would be drifting all over the place, blowing into the doors and through the windows and down the cistern. They'd drive us out of house and home if we gave them a chance. This is the third time I have raked the lawn this fall, and it's only a beginning. There's always more. But the only thing to do is to rake and burn them.'

After this fully explanatory outburst the man bent again to his sibilant labor, as though he had forgotten my presence. He was racing with the dark, which also was in the league against him, and had no more time to waste upon an idle sentimentalist who did not know what to do with leaves. Something wild in me bowed before the accumulated wisdom of centuries which makes good householders, trim lawns, and peaceful neighbors. The rambler was silenced, as usual, by the citizen. But though the rambler cannot answer back, knowing instinctively as well as by experience that most of the good arguments are against him, yet nothing can prevent him from thinking his thoughts. While good citizens are raking their leaves he may at least indulge his autumnal dreams.

I thought of Bunyan's Man with the Muck-rake, over whose head was held a celestial crown, but 'he did neither look up nor regard, but raked to himself the straws, the small sticks and the dust of the floor.' This man before me, this eminently respectable citizen, could not see even the beauty that lay before his eyes. I made him the symbol of all the barbarian millions to whom the little beauty they have left about them is a trouble and a perplexity, a dull ache which they cannot explain or wholly cure. This man felt impoverished, like Midas, by too much gold.

While I watched him rolling the wealth of Pactolus into piles and stuffing into gunny-sacks armfuls of sunset, I repented, for once, my free and foot-loose condition. Happy and homeless wanderer as I was for the nonce, I saw that the citizen, the householder, has this one advantage: he can entertain his leafy friends, if he will, at his own fireside.

To have a house of one's own, and there to be always at home to the leaves! And there rose up before me at once a house of dream set deep under mighty trees. Branches of elm and sycamore brushed its roof and waved along its shadowy gables. Great beeches and oaks thronged the yard, filling the air with flying leaves and strewing the grass with rustling gold and scarlet. And every door and window of the house stood wide open for these children of the wind to enter. Thither came ten thousand creatures that had burgeoned about my eaves and had made music for me through many a summer midnight. As soon as they were free to float and run they came dancing in crowds to the only home they knew, and they were made welcome. I kept an open house for leaves in autumn. By what right acknowledged among gentle beings could I have excluded them? For many months I had lived among them, watching their dance against the sky and listening to their voices; I had long enjoyed their hospitality, and now they had need of mine. It is true that they could not have put me out of their great house of swinging branches, and that I, on the contrary, had it in my power at any moment to seize a broom and send them scuttling out of my home; but I did not use that power. There are such differences as that, among others, between the rambler and the respectable citizen.

So the leaves came and stayed in my dream-built

house. They twirled and floated to the window-sill, hesitated a moment as though not sure of a welcome, and then vaulted into the rooms. They ran in breathless companies through the open doors, they explored the passages, brightened the window-seats with vivid hues, lay along the bookshelves, and over all the floor they sprawled in heaps. Was it their house or mine? We were a company of friends, and did not ask the question. However it may be with citizens, the rambler can never get too close to trees, and that is one reason why he does not take kindly to four walls and a roof. But give him a house where he can entertain maples and oaks and elms . . . then he is at home.

With such a house I endowed myself while the Man with the Rake denuded his lawn of beauty as best he could on the edge of nightfall. Thus we made our leaf-harvest, he and I.

INAMORATA

THE mountain pine is a man at arms
  With flashing shield and blade,
The willow is a dowager,
  The birch is a guileless maid,
But the elm tree is a lady
  In gold and green brocade.

Broad-bosomed to the meadow breeze
  The matron maple grows,
The poplar plays the courtesan
  To every wind that blows,
But who the tall elm's lovers are
  Only the midnight knows.

And few would ever ask it
  Of such a stately tree,
So lofty in the moonlight,
  So virginal stands she,
Snaring the little silver fish
  That swim her silent sea.

But hush! A hum of instruments
  Deep in the night begins;
Along those dusky galleries
  Low music throbs and thins —
A whispering of harps and flutes
  And ghostly violins.

For what mysterious visitor
  Do all her windy bells
Ring welcome in the moonlight
  And amorous farewells?

.   .   .   .   .   .

The elm tree is a lady.
  The midnight never tells.

DISTANT MUSIC

ELM branches,
Swaying,
Balancing a million leaves
Against a cloud of silver,
What magic in your dreamy dip-and-toss?
What meaning in your mystic to-and-fro?

A fragrance from the hills of youth
Sweeps through these swinging boughs . . .
Some distant music
That has lived long upon the edge of silence.

Some door is opened out of long ago.
Faces look forth from long-forgotten windows.
Faint calls I hear,
Echoes,
And fainter answers,
Across the fields of childhood.

Ah! they were very fair, those fields, those faces,
All changeless now,
All safe and beautiful forever,
Shining like clouds above the hills of sunrise
With early light upon them.

Ye bring me back the golden afternoons
Of some slow-smouldering October,
Elm branches,
Majestically swaying,
Brushing the shadowed doorways of remembrance.

XII
MOTHER EARTH

Fear not the new generalization. Does the fact look crass and material, threatening to degrade thy theory of spirit? Resist it not; it goes to refine and raise thy theory of matter just as much.
— EMERSON

Raise the stone, and there ye shall find me. Cleave the wood, and there am I also.
— *Oxyrhyncus Papyri*

 ON the morning after my return to Salisbury I shouldered my knapsack again and set forth toward the town of Canaan. But I did not get so far. Near the top of Wells Hill I came to a huge white pine that grew between the road and the stone wall, its roots making a natural chair, and I sat down there to think out some of the hints that had come to me in yesterday's musings. I sat there for several hours, looking at the quiet landscape before me, listening to the wind in the pine boughs, and writing now and then upon scraps of paper. This is what I wrote:

Down the slope before me lies a little meadow surrounded by a shad fence and containing nine elms, two ash trees, and one brindled cow. Beyond this is a farmyard, and on the horizon above it looms the long wooded height of Mount Prospect. Looking to the left across the lane that runs beside me, I catch glimpses through the leaves of Bear Mountain guarding the northwest corner of Connecticut. The morning sun strikes down a warm beam upon me, though it has a core of autumnal coolness. Flocks of wool-pack clouds are driving before the west wind, their shadows incessantly climbing and descending the slopes to northward — now spreading over a thousand acres of tilted woodland, blotting all their gold and crimson into blue, and then slowly moving on, leaving the brave colors of maple and hickory even brighter than before, as though they had been washed in shadow. The solid hills flash and darken so that they seem, like the highest clouds of sunrise, to have only enough substance to hold their hues together. Made of granite and mould as they are, I can almost believe that they are immaterial, and the sunshine sweeping over them after the shadow's passing has the effect of a smile on a human face.

I have watched the changing hills for an hour in great content, with hardly a thought of any kind, wholly absorbed and thrust forth in the act of seeing. Tired for a moment of this panorama, I have found an equal pleasure in watching an ant that has been toiling the whole time over and among the pine needles at my feet, his red body almost transparent in the sunshine and his nervous antennæ picked out clear against the mould. I have seen a downy woodpecker climb a stem of scarlet woodbine beside the stone wall exactly as a

sailor swarms up a rope. Two sadly faded bluebirds perched upon the wall have been eyeing me steadily for five minutes, turning their heads through half circles to observe me first with one eye and then with the other. I have never been more exhaustively scrutinized even by European peasants amazed at American clothes. Do they see the physical man with one eye and my character with the other? . . . I have just thrown a cone at them and made them fly away.

Now here, at last, is an experience worth recording: Two minutes after the departure of the bluebirds I heard a sudden alarum down the slope, like the stutter of a rapid-fire gun, and immediately after I saw a Chinese pheasant in full regalia running through the little field, his hen following behind like an obsequious shadow. In a moment he took wing and came up the slope directly toward me, lifting his gorgeous tail over the wall in a magnificent parabola and alighting in the road ten feet away, the hen following his example. I sat as still as the pine trunk behind me while they moved in and out over the wavering sun-spots, as much at ease as chickens in a barnyard. But I had less than a minute to think how strange it was that these two splendid creatures from Cathay should be feeding beside me in a Connecticut lane before the wild black eye of the cock discovered me, and then — the English language does not serve to make clear what happened, and I borrow Cicero's words about the abrupt departure of Catiline — '*abiit, excessit, evasit, erupit.*' As for the hen, although I did not see her go, the place where she had been was observed to be vacant. 'Splendor fell from the day.'

I can hear a bevy of goldfinches among the thistles over the wall, and a nuthatch enlivens the morning with his nasal baritone. In the little twittering birch half way down the hill a chickadee is performing prodigies of ground-and-lofty tumbling. Thus, without any apparent effort, the small people of the wayside manage to keep me mildly amused. My inquisitive friend the chipmunk, who resides somewhere in the wall, would be enough by himself alone to prevent the time from hanging heavy on my hands. With manners superior to those of the bluebirds, he is quite as curious as they, pretending to busy himself with this and that trifle among the grasses but really observing me steadily all the while. Now and then he disappears among the stones, but a moment later I discover his tiny head projecting from another crevice in the wall, his beady eye fixed upon me in almost passionate interrogation. Just now he is sitting back on his haunches and talking at me with a vehemence and volubility that shakes him all over.

In trying to explain the happiness I have had here under the pine tree, I have been thinking over the idea that I grazed the edge of yesterday as I walked up the Housatonic — the idea that picturesque beauty in landscape is only the rouge on Nature's cheek, an external gaud or flourish which her true lovers can do without. The beauty that I see before me is hardly such as a superficial glance would discover. It is like that of a plain and long familiar face on which the years have written patience and gentleness and kindly wisdom, a face beloved all the more because it does not amaze or ravish us. If all the haste and morbid intensity had not been worn out of me by my fortnight of walking in the open, I should hardly see or feel it at all; yet this is not to say that it is negligible. The few celebrated landscapes that I have seen have not meant so much to me as this little scene at which I am looking now, this meadow with its nine elms, and two ash trees, and brindled cow, and the long wooded height of Mount Prospect beyond. I think, indeed, that my ever-deepening love of Connecticut must be partly due to this, that it shows nearly everywhere a beauty that invites my collaboration and seems to need my human comment — a beauty, in short, that can be harvested only by a quiet eye.

Whether this love of the earth for its own sufficient sake, apart from any 'lust of the eye,' is a common thing or very rare, I have never been able to make sure. Literature does not record it clearly, perhaps because it is too elemental for direct expression: one can only say that it is not this and is not that. Yet it seems almost certain that Thoreau, with his life-long devotion to the modest meadows of Concord, would have understood me. And Emerson too understood, else he could never have written the words that have come back to me so many times during these two weeks: 'Crossing a bare common, in snow-puddles, at twilight, under a clouded sky, I am glad to the brink of fear.' Thoreau and Emerson — it is already impossible to compute what we owe to these two New England prophets who learned the lesson of earth so thoroughly and taught it to a few others so effectively just because their Concord was little and obscure and unremarkable. Concord taught them what Connecticut is continually teaching me, that the really devout can worship at least as well in a temple swept bare of adornment as in sculptured and vividly colored cathedral aisles.

Brown earth, bare rocks, a leaden pool, even the firm rough bark of an oak as I pass my hand over it, the smell of sawn timber, the smell of wood-smoke on a frosty morning, a note of brook-song, a maple in October or a flowering cherry in late April, elm boughs waving against the sky — any one of these things, or of ten thousand other things equally simple, is enough, now, to waken the thrill of devotion and of awe. And I can go farther still — to the verge, or beyond it, of what would seem absurdity to one who has never known this ascetic love of earth. Holding my left hand up, just now, against the sunbeam, I saw a delicate edging of shell-pink along the fingers, with graduated tones of red deepening toward the palm, and there swept over me exactly the same thrill of wonder and awe that all men feel in the presence of earth's more celebrated mysteries. Delight in the mere beauty of color played some part, no doubt, in that little experience, but I should prefer to call the strange pleasure it gave me a kind of adoration.   For my hand was Nature too, as much as yonder mountain, and just as subject to 'the one Spirit's plastic stress,' the streams and tides that moved in it no less marvelous than those that roll from shore to shore of the Atlantic. But it might as well have been a maple leaf that gave me this sudden reverential impulse, or the wing-case of a beetle, or a faded bluebird feather.

This impulse came to me more overpoweringly than ever before or ever since, I remember — how vividly I remember! — fifteen years ago on a sea-beach in Southern California, while I sat in the sunshine and sifted the dry golden grains of sand between my fingers. Suddenly I seemed to understand, as in a flash of inspiration, that these sand-grains, each a world in itself and each charged with all the forces of the universe, brought me as near as I had ever been or could hope to go to the Divine. In that moment of exaltation, or of fatuity, I singled out one grain of translucent quartz and held it in my palm for the sun to strike through, saying to myself that here was all, quite all, that science probes and poets sing and saints adore.

If this was mere fatuity, I should like to know why such flashes of what seems like insight come to me only on the best of my days, after weeks of soberly joyous living have brought me into accord, body and mind and soul, with the triune world. On such days, and on such only, the plucking of any string sets the whole instrument into sympathetic vibration. Then it is that almost any chance-chosen particle of the

infinite world — a human face, an air from Mozart,
a grain of sand — seems to tremble with the splendor
and power of the Whole. How can I reject the revelation that comes when I am living as a whole man and
accept the partial glimpses of one-third men — the
sensualist, the scholar, and the saint? One knows what
things he has seen during the instantaneous flash of
lightning, even though his may be the only eye that
sees them; and when the flash is past . . . well, 'let us
not deny in the darkness the things we have seen in
the light.'

These twenty Christian centuries, so-called, have
been a lonely time for those who have striven for the
higher health or wholeness. First the ascetic began to
'fiddle harmonics' upon a single string, and perhaps
the most important of his accomplishments was to
teach the thinker and the sensualist to do the same —
since when we have had strange music. In their
anæmic and fine-lady fear of the flesh Christians have
effeminized the supreme human figure of Jesus out of
all recognition, making him sexless, bloodless, passion-
less, unfit for any man's following or any woman's love,
as though striving to cancel that vastly significant
mystery of the Incarnation which lies at the core of
their creed. Body and brain have taken their revenge
by raising themselves separately into the same isolation claimed by the spirit, attaining crass brutality
on the one hand and arid intellectualism on the other.
To-day, therefore, the main task of religion and education alike — a task not yet begun or even recognized —

is simply to restore men and women to the unity of
their powers.

The readiest way to set about this task is to restore
in men and women that basic and primitive yet exalted
love of earth in which the senses and the mind and the
spirit come together. Do we not already see that whenever we bring any one of these three intensely to bear
upon 'Nature' the other two are soon called in to help
it out? Consider the example offered by natural science.
Obviously enough it has sharpened and disciplined the
senses, but what of the spirit? Many have said — and,
alas! many are still saying — that here its effect has
been to dwarf and cripple. On the contrary, the influence of natural science, even in these its infant days,
is already a powerfully spiritual influence. So far from
destroying or laying waste, it enormously extends the
realms of wonder and of beauty, revealing more mar-
vels in a lump of mud than theology has ever surmised
in the stars. Like the poet, natural science packs the
universe so full of spirit that there is no room left for
anything dull or foul or base. I often think that it is
making steadily, in its surer-footed way, toward those
same conclusions to which I have leaped but which I
cannot prove or even clearly describe without its help.
The walls that seem to separate matter from mind, and
both of these from spirit — walls that are raised and
maintained, I believe, only by the habits of our own
thinking — are already thin.   I can hear the scientist
striking tremendous blows on the other side of the
wall along which I grope and fumble. Some day we
shall stand face to face.

Such a movement 'back to Nature' as I have in mind would stand a better chance of success than that recently led by sentimental 'view-hunters' and by prattlers about the 'simple life,' for its main concern would be to raise human beings once more to their normal stature, to substitute whole men and women for the maimed and writhen creatures that we are. It would not need to work any radical change in us, for the love of earth is already wellnigh universal, as it is incalculably ancient. We know that it is very old and very wide-spread because it is woven into nearly all religions. Christianity almost alone has been against it, waging long and indecisive war against the earth deities. Only a few of the boldest Christian minds, apparently, have seen how spirit and mind and matter mesh and interpenetrate. Only a few, and they unheard or misunderstood, have realized that hatred and fear of the flesh, exemplified in every Christian age from Saint Anthony to Anthony Comstock, is at bottom an enormous blasphemy.

Yet our instinctive love of earth lies still very near the surface of our thought, and it may well outlast the creeds whose age, in comparison, is of yesterday. Our children may return to a religion of earth constructed not by theologians but by scientists and poets and holy men working together upon the foundations of this universal instinct. The old theology is fast crumbling away, but there is little likelihood that religion will crumble with it. Our time may be remembered not as the epoch during which an old faith perished but as that in which a new faith, incorporating the best of the old upon a deeper, sounder base, struggled slowly into being.

The gulf between spirit and matter seems so wide and deep that we cannot conceive how it is ever to be bridged; but neither can we conceive how the flint gives birth to a spark of fire or how the tremendous gap is leaped between black marks on white paper and knowledge, thought, emotion. We do not understand how the violinist draws dreams out of horsehair and catgut; we merely observe that he does so. The gulf, after all, is of our own digging, and Nature knows nothing of it. Mother Earth knows nothing of the petty distinctions we set up between things 'noble' and 'base.' When we have learned to think more respectfully of her we shall remember that the rose as well as the cabbage is her child, that Shelley's Odes and the visions of Saint Theresa have exactly the same source as the potato. Beethoven's symphonies, if we will allow ourselves to think of it, were made in part of bread and cheese and beer. Is this thought degrading to the music? Rather, it should suggest a reason for thinking better of beer and bread and cheese than we are accustomed to think. . . . Ah, no! Some day we shall abandon this childish effort to find a flower without a root, to make music without an instrument, to save our souls without saving our bodies too. The earth that bore us and taught us all we know calls in our very blood. Some day we shall go home to her.

It is related in Plutarch's Moralia that the pilot Thamus, while sailing near the Isle of Paxi, heard a vast voice proclaiming to the sky and sea: 'Great Pan is dead!' As this proclamation was made during the reign of Tiberius, it was to early Christians as an abdication of the elder gods in favor of the young god of Palestine. For eighteen centuries the priests have been exulting over the dead God Pan, and the poets have mourned him as lost forever to the fields and the forest. Perhaps it is presumptuous in me, an idle vagabond dreaming the noon away under the pine boughs, to doubt this almost unanimous testimony of those who ought to know, but the fact that I have just followed the unmistakable paths of Pan along three boundaries of Connecticut may give me the right to a minority opinion. I make bold to say, therefore, that he is not dead so long as even one worshiper walks reverently in his temple, alert in body and mind and soul, giving to each its due. I know that I am not worthy, yet I should wish to be his worshiper even if I had to be the last.

If Pan were really dead, then we should have to revive him; for we cannot do without his rough male strength, all hirsute and half-hircine as he is, to remind us that religion is something different from social respectability. Had he not long since shaken the dust of our churches from his shaggy hooves, the religion of the western world might now be a lovelier and livelier thing. To say that he is the arch-foe of Puritania is not to admit, what some confidently assert, that he is the

Devil masquerading under another name. His enemies have insisted upon his animal nature — and indeed he is a splendid animal, naked and unashamed — but they have forgotten that he instructed Apollo himself in prophecy. They have had much to say about his disreputable companions, Silenus and Priapus, but they do not tell us how he put the whole host of Titans to

flight, thereby winning the day for Olympus, by a single blast of his terrible trumpet. They relate that he frightened his mother in the hour of his birth, but not that he charmed the young Dionysus and made music out of sorrow with the reed that had been Syrinx. And finally, they have made nothing of this most engaging of all his traits, that he loves the earth with an entire and passionate devotion — that he is, indeed, the very voice and personification of the earth, violent and tender, sad and joyous, dreamy and down-right, and above all poetic. Although he was intro-duced by his father to the shining companies of Olym-pus, he returned at once to the earth, to the shepherds and huntsmen and fishermen whom he understood and who still, in some measure, understand him. That, I think, is the surest sign of his true godhead: when given his choice between them, he preferred the earth to heaven. Those many gods who chose to remain in the sky may be there even now for aught we know, or care; but Pan still walks the earth. Under one or an-other of his thousand names, he will always have wor-shipers. It may be that his greater glory is yet to come.

I am well aware that in saying these things I lay myself open to the gravest misinterpretation, for in this territory a hair divides the true from the false. I know very well the danger pointed out by George Santayana: 'In casting off with self-assurance and a sense of fresh vitality the distinctions of tradition and reason, a man may feel, as he sinks comfortably back to a lower level of sense and instinct, that he is returning to Nature or escaping into the infinite. Mysticism makes us proud and happy to renounce the work of intelligence, both in thought and in life, and persuades us that we become divine by remaining imperfectly human.' Further-more, I know that the sense of kinship or identity with

earth may lead, and often has led, to ignoble ends
when it means, as with Walt Whitman, merely a limp
'sinking down into the landscape.' I wish to distinguish my thought very sharply from the sentimental
and romantic mood expressed by Heinrich Heine:
*'Unendlich selig ist das Gefühl, wenn die Erschein-
ungswelt mit unserer Gemütswelt zuzammenrinnt,
und grüne Bäume, Gedanken, Vögelgesang, Wehmut,
Himmelsbläue, Erinnerung, und Kräuterduft sich in
süszen Arabesken verschlingen.'* Here we see thought
submerged by the senses and a human mind lapsing
toward the animal. The only 'happiness' that I can
imagine in this sort of thing is that of falling asleep,
but the happiness I find in my experience is that of un-
accustomed alertness. During the hours I have spent
here on Wells Hill my thoughts and memories have
not become entangled with the trees and the odors
of the fields and the blue of the sky; rather I should
say that I have taken all these things up into myself
and that they have been thinking and feeling through
me. So far as these words are concerned, or any other
words that I might find, this may seem to be a distinction without a difference, yet I know that the difference
is really profound. It is the difference, indeed, between
a passive and an active mood. I admit that when I
began my walk, two weeks ago, at Brooklyn, I took
whatever came and was glad enough to let my thoughts
simply bask in the sun, for then I was a tired man; but
more and more, as the miles and the days have gone
by, I have resumed control, until now I seem in some

sense to create the landscape as I go along. I am no
longer a mere bundle of traveling senses, but rather
Francis Bacon's *Homo additus Naturæ*. Prospect
Mountain over yonder is not merely a thing to be
looked at: it is also a thought. I find that I cannot
put my whole meaning into clearer words than these,
but that is no reason why I should distrust the exulta-
tion, celebrated by Santayana himself, which is felt
'when the mind and the world are knit in a brief embrace,' when earth is transfigured by human thought
and Nature is raised to the human level.

One who lives in his faith may have a higher vision
and a deeper serenity than any that I am acquainted
with among the Connecticut Calvinists — barring such
men of religious genius as Jonathan Edwards — who
once ruled all this land that I look out across. My
theology is far less definite, my notions of good and evil
are much less precise, than theirs; they were quite
certain about many things which I am content to leave
in the shadow of mystery; they derived from their
doctrine an iron discipline of will and reason which I
shall never be able to find in mine; and yet I do not
bow before them as my spiritual superiors. I can praise
them for many things, but not for this, that they were
strangers in the fair world where I am every year more
and more at home. I cannot praise the love of God
that expresses itself in contempt for God's fair handi-
work. If we may trust their own account, they knew
pathetically little about simple happiness: I have

spelled some words in its primer. They had a keener
and more abiding sense than I of a God outside the
world He made: I have a keener sense than they of a
God inside that world. They looked back upon a
Revelation completed long ago: I look out upon a
Revelation now in progress, never to be complete. . . .
These are some of the differences to be considered in a
preliminary test of the religion of earth. Of course I
know while I write them down that if one of their
mighty men, say Cotton Mather or Richard Hooker
or Thomas Shepard, should come up the road just now
to discuss these questions, he could cite a thousand
texts to confuse and entangle me; but the logic of the
heart would be against him.

The sun is descending now upon the summit of
Mount Riga, and the colors of the hills are deepened
as he goes down the sky. The evening of my last day
in the country is drawing in. What, now, shall I save
to remember out of this final day and out of the two
golden weeks to which it has been the appropriately
quiet climax and close? Colors of sunrise and sunset,
colors of trees, the song of the wind through the pine
— a thousand sights and sounds. But even more than
these things I should like to remember my present
thought or mood as the goal of my fortnight's wandering. Free for a few hours yet from the clutch of cir-
cumstance, glad for the days that have been and
gladly facing the days to come, I sit here in the last
rays of the sun fulfilled with such a love of the brown

earth, my Mother, as I have seldom known before. And it comes to me, as I sit here in this devotion of quiet thought, that all the vast toil of Nature struggling upward to this moment has here reached one of its terms. Earth sees now, through my eyes, the vision of her own beauty. Earth knows herself at last, and knows that she is divine.

VESPERS

TWILIGHT falls on the hill.
The west is a crumble of sundown.
From hollow and cavern and cranny
The shadows lengthen and creep.
And a slow singing of far bells
Blows on the breath of the evening
From the dim-piled crepuscular mountains
And intricate valleys of sleep.

Lamp after lamp shines forth
From the scattered farm windows below me.
A lantern moves by the rick.
Cattle low at the bars.
Comes the dull rumble of barn doors.
Voices of weary children
Dwindle into the dusk. . . .
Night — and the stars!

God, if thou grantest me Heaven,
Take not this beauty from me,
But down from the lonely sky
Send thou my spirit again,
Back to the old worn ways
Of this little flickering planet —
Back to the grief and the toil
And the hopes and the homes of men.

XIII

TWO-TWENTY-THREE

To-morrow let the Great Father fill the sky with black cloud or with sunshine; He shall not thereby make vain what is past, nor undo and wipe out what the flying hour has brought.

— HORACE

 ALL night I had heard a breeze from the west fingering the elm-tops, and looking out in the small hours I saw ·the stars shining bright after their bath in a day-long rain; but when the dawn came to Salisbury over Prospect Mountain the wind suddenly veered and grew until it came booming out of the northern Berkshires with flocks of dazzling cloud before it. Another walking day! The oak leaves beside my window glittered like split emerald.

Before breakfast I made my farewell visits — to a little hill where the pine boughs were silvering in the wind, to one or two pools in the mill-brook, and to the mill itself. There I found the door already open, with sunlight slanting in upon the powdered floor and glorifying the festoons of creamy cobwebs hanging from every beam and rafter. Already the wheels were grinding. I shouted good-morning to the young miller, whose face and coat were creamy-gold with corn-dust,

and conversed with him as best I could over the din of
the falls. He said that the milling business was not
what it had been in his father's time; yet I gathered
that he expected to spend his life here among the cobwebs and the noise of rushing water, and I thought I
had known a good many young men with gloomier
prospects. At twenty he knew all the craft of milling,
and he could look forward to sixty years of collaboration with the sun and the earth and the mountain. Of
course his gains would be very small, because only the
wasteful work that had better not be done at all is
highly paid in this ingeniously ordered world, and he
would be doing only one of those indispensable tasks
for which we pay what is called 'a living wage.' But
it seemed that he might secure at least the wages of
happiness. I caught myself almost envying the future
he might have there, lulled by the year-long thunder of
the stream.

Shortly after nine o'clock, I set out on the eighteen-
mile walk to Norfolk, where I was to catch the east-
bound train at two-twenty-three. Considering that I
did not know the way and that a good part of my road
must run through rugged country, I saw that this last
day would be a test of my pedestrianism. Hitherto I
had walked with a cheerful contempt of time-tables,
trying only to arrive at some house of entertainment
before the cook had gone to bed; but now I was returning to civilization — to side-walks, stiff collars, tele-
phones, bill-boards, electric gongs, clock-punchers,

steam whistles, claxons, traffic policemen, fire engines, hurdy-gurdies, player pianos, radio sets, Sunday supplements — and the symbol of this return echoed

everlastingly in my brain all the way to Norfolk: '2.23, two-twenty-three, Two-Twenty-Three, *TWO–TWENTY– THREE.*'

Could I make it? Old habits of mind swept back over me, and I divided the intervening minutes into a rough schedule, determining to walk as nearly four miles an hour as possible, to spend not more than fifteen minutes at lunch, and so to save some leeway for making inquiries about the road and for getting lost. Time, which had been for two weeks the raw material of happiness, became a mere coin which I was forced to spend in a dictated way for a commodity I did not really want. Yesterday I had sat for five hours under a pine tree on Wells Hill, watching cloud-shadows and jotting down random thoughts — an occupation recognizably human. To-day I was merely a minute particle once more in the world-machine, dragged irresistibly over eighteen miles of hill and vale to catch the two-twenty-three.

And yet, perhaps, not quite irresistibly. Even as I measured the distance against the time and struck into the four-mile pace, feeling the load of the world's mostly futile labor settle down again upon my shoulders, a faint voice deep down in me seemed to say that I was still a free man, acting as such, that I could go or stay as I  chose, and that therefore I was setting forth to catch the two-twenty-three, with all the ludicrous corollaries that this implied, because in some sense I wanted to. We have all heard that voice, and none of us can say with assurance whether it lies or tells the truth. On the day before, if the question had occurred to me, I should have found some 'hill retired,' like Milton's philosophers, and there I should have

> reasoned high
> Of Providence, Foreknowledge, Will, and Fate —
> Fixed fate, free will, foreknowledge absolute —
> And found no end, in wandering mazes lost.

But now, sucked back into the maëlstrom, I was called upon, as we say, to 'act'; my time was gone by for finding an intelligent reason for action and for asking whether, after all, any man can act quite freely. I can only say, therefore, that on this day, if I was a free man, I behaved strangely like an automaton.

Striding through Salisbury Vale toward Norfolk and the twentieth century, I amused myself with romantic fancies of escape. How easy and natural it would be, I thought, instead of marching straight onward, to turn north into the Berkshires, or south into unexplored Connecticut, and then, having made this minute decision, just to keep on going! As for the tiny part of 'the world's work' that I should be leaving, such a course would make room for another man more earnest and skilful, because more sure of the work's value, than I. For a few people — it was a pleasure to count and name them over — my disappearance would for a time take something out of life, and for a very few it would mean a permanent sorrow. But on the other hand there were others — I would not stop to count them — to whom my departure would be a relief. The people, I said, who think somewhat as I do have nothing to learn from me, and those who think otherwise *will* learn nothing either from my argument or my opposition. I had worked rather hard in the world for a number of years, earning what the world can give in excitement, knowledge, love and hate, aspiration and failure, so that from now on to the end I could expect little but repetition. Though the best years lay ahead, I was persuaded, the question was open how I could best use them. I had come to the time in life when the wise men of India, having fulfilled their duties to the state and to

society, begin to think of themselves, retiring into
their own minds and enjoying at last the only true goal
of work, which is leisure. How stupid, I thought, is our
religion of the strenuous life beside their art of living!
How puerile is such a symbol of our view as the picture
of Russell Sage at seventy-six bending over a stock-
ticker beside their Books of Forest Wisdom!

I found a strange pleasure in thinking how little
difference my disappearance would make, and in
quoting:

> When you and I behind the veil are past,
> Oh, but the long long while the world shall last,
>   Which of our coming and departure heeds
> As the Seven Seas should heed a pebble-cast.

Why a man with a normal allowance of *amour propre*
should take delight in such considerations I do not
know, unless because he thinks that part of him which
'the world's coarse thumb and finger' has appraised at
slight value is not the essential part. All I can say is
that it amused me to imagine certain lecture halls
where audiences would await my coming for perhaps a
quarter of an hour and then disband, with their dis-
appointment under excellent control. . . .

> Et interrogatum est ab omnibus:
>   'Ubi est ille Toad-in-the-hole?'
> Et responsum est ab omnibus:
>   'Non est inventus.'

I thought of the committees that would convene with
one of their members over the hills and far away, and of
how one or two ideas that I had fought for, established,

and upheld by my own strength would go down very soon to defeat . . . and I knew that it would not matter.

READER — Try as you may to conceal it, all this is unpleasantly egotistical.

WRITER — But surely, in a man's own book . . . And besides, what I am telling you seems to me a curious fact about our common human nature. Here was I, after two weeks of perfect freedom to go where I liked, to feel and think and say what I liked, racing back to thrust my head again into the halter; yet all the while I had the feeling that I was free. You may be able to explain this quite easily, but if so you are wiser than I am. And you will please to remember that all the while I **was** thinking these things, flattering the vagabond in me with dreams of moonlit haystacks and of little fires beneath blackened pails, I was making four miles an hour over the hills toward the two-twenty-three.

Before eleven o'clock I was standing on the bridge at Falls Village, studying the map, which gave me such a perplexing tangle of routes leading to Norfolk that I decided to ask for instruction. Entering an inn near the bridge, I called for an undesired glass of ginger ale — which turned out to be entirely undesirable — and pumped the landlord, while I pretended to drink, with questions about the road. His directions, illustrated by a wet finger on the bar, were so circumstantial that I almost believed the final ominous formula: 'You can't miss it.' But the graveyard of which he had made so much did not come to view in all the long-drawn-out village. Seeing, however, that I was at least walking eastward, I went on for a mile or so, until I came to a house by a cross-roads and heard from behind it the sound of an ax thudding fee-bly upon soft wood. There I found a man of almost eighty, in overcoat and muffler, at work upon his winter wood pile. He had heard of a road over Canaan Moun-tain, and had actually  traveled it some sixty years before, but when I found that he could not recall the name of the county I gave little heed to his directions. The best thing he told me was that I might go 'daown the road a piece till I came to Old Bill Haowe's place,' and there I could inquire again.

Bill Howe I found in his back yard, also chopping wood, and he was wearing galoshes. (The old people of Falls Village take no chances on the weather.) Apparently he had never heard of Canaan Mountain, which frowned down upon him while he spoke. Such ignorance as this would be an interesting phenomenon to a man with time to enjoy it, but it must be that I

betrayed some impatience, because he took refuge in
the trick of all stupid men and called his wife. Her
stupidity, quite equal to his, was aggravated by a
paralyzed tongue, one of the rarest of feminine afflic-
tions. When I asked her about the road over Canaan
Mountain into Norfolk she asserted: 'You go' 'o go 'o
'or' Ca'aa'.' I protested that North Canaan would
take me twenty miles out of my way and that I knew
there was a direct road. She repeated her statement,
doggedly, woodenly, without a lingual. But when she
had made this remark for the third time and I still de-
murred, Bill broke in with his only sensible suggestion:
'Call Smittie.' She did so.

'Clump — Clump — Clump,' sounded heavy boots
on an inner stair, and Smittie emerged smiling into the
sunlight. He was a wiry little man, forty years old, not
more than five feet in height, with the purest Yankee
face I have ever seen . . . a face that had been sharpened
for three centuries on Connecticut boulders. One could
see that his wits had been sharpened at the same time,
for the light that danced in his brown eyes was token of
a fine natural intelligence. Although his clothing was
coarse and his small hands were already twisted and
old, there was a wild beauty about the man that went
to the heart. His dusty brown hair with a glint of gold,
his square jaw, broad shoulders, narrow waist, proud
and sensitive nose, but most of all something at once
eager and sad in his eyes, made me think of him as a
John Keats in blue overalls.

Smittie had heard about Canaan Mountain. Indeed,

he made it seem that he must have invented it, for his directions were a model of simple clarity. He drew a picture of the mountain in the air with his hands, laid down upon that picture a map of the road I should follow, wafting me upward in fancy with his left hand while drawing with his right, and climbing an imaginary mountain all the time with his feet. It was a lively pantomime, ludicrous and yet somehow beautiful, with a touch of pathos that I  could not explain. Smittie talked with his whole body, with his face and eyes, as well as with his tongue — which had itself extraordinary skill in a speech as swift and expressive as it was ungrammatical. He gave himself up entirely to his listener, and thus contrasted even more sharply with the silent and sluggish Howes.

Here was one of the few New-Englanders who have a natural gift for rich and voluble expression. What racial explanation there may have been for him I could not say, for his name told me nothing; but his diminutive stature, his auburn hair and eyes, and something in the shape of his head made me suspect that he was a reversion, strangely encountered on this Connecticut hillside, to the Celtic type. Although he had been long enough in New England to acquire the sharp features and nasal twang of the Yankee — and that could not be done in less than two hundred years — he derived ultimately, I guessed, from the oldest inhabitants of Cornwall — the people who used to show visiting Phœnicians the way over their hills, the people from whom John Keats himself may have sprung.

Smittie described my route for me three times over, with manifest enjoyment, beaming happily up at me out of his hazel eyes. And then, when I was going, he said:

'It's a fine day for walkin'. You'll get right smart of a breeze on top o' the maountin, I expect.'

A suggestion of wistfulness in his tone half revealed the secret of his delight in the foregoing pantomime. Had he been taking my walk with me in imaginary anticipation, feeling how I should enjoy it? Perhaps this was the reason why he had lifted his feet so high, like a man scrambling up a steep incline. I closed the gate I had half opened and turned to Smittie again.

'How far is it,' I said, 'to Norfolk?'

His face fell at this, and the light in his eyes went out. 'O Lord!' he sighed; 'I don't know. I never *was* to Norfork.'

'You have never been to Norfolk! Then how do you know the way so well?'

'Oh,' said he, 'I just heard folks tell.'

Smittie had been posing as a first-hand authority, and now he had to climb down into a mere middle-man of learning. Here was the rough outline of a little tragedy.

'How long have you been living here?' I asked him.

'Born here,' he said. 'Just daown the road a little piece.'

'And yet you have never been to Norfolk! Well, it's a fine town, I can tell you. Much bigger than Falls Village.'

'Yes; so they do say.'

'Well, then, suppose you come along and go with me, right away now.'

Although he was more pleased than I liked to see by this invitation, I repented at once that I had made it. 'I wisht I could,' he said; 'but I gotta work. Mr. Haowe, he wouldn't let me off. Good-bye!' . . . and he began again his illustrated directions as I let myself out at the rusty gate.

'Mr. Haowe, he wouldn't let me off.' That sentence revealed the fact, to me almost shocking, that Smittie was the hired servant in this household. Smittie, the descendant of Cornish kings and Welsh bards — in my sympathy I felt quite sure of this — at the beck and call of two people whose ancestors must always have been the dullest of yokels! He had a hundred times their combined intelligence; but also — and this may have been the explanation — he had a guileless heart. He made me think of Sterne's caged starling and its pathetic cry: 'I can't get out! I can't get out!'

Smittie had told me that after crossing a certain valley I should ascend through an orchard toward a white pine that stands conspicuously on the hillside. I did so, thereby saving half a mile, and found my road there climbing determinedly uphill. There is a saying in these parts that a man driving down this mountain road never sees his horse over the dashboard from the time he leaves the top until he reaches the valley. The only thing I noticed particularly about the road was that it kept on climbing long after it might reasonably have been expected to stop. But I was in haste.

To speak more exactly, I was in great haste. Two hours before I had been toying with the question whether it was worth while to catch my train; but now, when I began to think it impossible, all my future happiness seemed to depend upon my doing so. I had been walking swiftly; now I began to hurry — a different and much more exhausting thing. I ran down every little decline and tried to maintain the four-mile-an-hour pace on the opposite slope. The more I hurried the more necessary, the more a matter of life-and-death it seemed that I should catch the two-twenty-three. However free to choose I may have been in the early morning, at noon I had no more freedom than a particle of iron-dust in the grip of a powerful magnet.

Yet I did assert my independence for a few minutes before taking the final plunge into modernity. On the top of Canaan Mountain there is a plateau with a few farms upon it and a wide road or common running its whole length. This common I found cluttered with cows in various attitudes of noon-tide rumination. They blocked my way. They gazed at me in mild astonishment, as though they had never seen a man in a hurry before. Stupid creatures they looked to me, and I could not understand how they had ever seemed beautiful — as they undoubtedly had only the day before. But somehow they reminded me of my uneaten lunch. I determined that I would not be sneered at by cows. It was just then that I came to a lonely school on the very top of the mountain, and in the school yard I saw a man sitting under a tree and reading a book. His example was even more persuasive than that of the cows. I walked across the yard and sat down beside him without ceremony, for I had no breath to ask permission. He did not resent the intrusion, however, but closed his book, slipped it into his pocket, and watched my simple preparations for luncheon.

'How far to Norfolk station?' I panted.

'Six miles,' said he.

Seeing that he was himself a rambler, I was sure that he knew the distance to a nicety and that he told the truth. And then he added, when he saw me glance at my watch: 'But it's nearly all downhill.'

That was a good hearing. I had left exactly an hour and a half. He would not accept any of my nuts and raisins, having just had his dinner at a farmhouse near at hand. We talked about the road I had come over that morning, which he knew very well, and I commended Smittie to his kindest attentions. This led on somehow to the poems of W. H. Davies which he had been reading and to the poetry of tramps and vagabonds generally. I named some books written by or about

tramps and hoboes that he had not heard of, and he did the same for me. He thought George Borrow the most interesting English prose-writer of the nineteenth century, and I did not dispute the opinion — partly because I was gathering energy for my final dash and partly because, at just that time and place, the opinion seemed possibly correct.

My companion became really interesting, however, when he said that this hill-top always reminded him of a place where he had camped once, years ago, in the Vosges. Thus I learned that he had seen service in the Great War, attaining the rank of Major and several decorations. What I learned further was more significant: that he had hated the whole business of soldiering with a mighty hatred while he was engaged in it, and more and more ever since as he gained the perspective of time; that his experience at the front had made him a thorough-going 'pacifist,' sceptical of nearly all patriotism and loathing all 'patrioteers.' Apparently I had tapped an inexhaustible vein of enthusiastic vituperation. He grew positively lyrical, and at the same time eloquently profane, in describing the game of war as he had known it — a game, he said, not originally, which is 'damned dangerous, damned dirty, and damned dull,' fit only for bad little boys and the lower savages. These were strong words, worth listening to only because they were based upon real experience; but he went on to say that he had been left by the War with no more affection for the country governed at Washington than he had for that governed at Berlin, or at Petrograd. What he did really love was this little circle of hills we looked out over, where he had been born and brought up. These hundred square miles he could imagine himself fighting for again. Also he would fight, if necessary, for the United States of the World, but not for any artificial and trumped-up country or cause in between those two.

This was a brave phraseology, to say the least, and in some ways it chimed so exactly with feelings of my own that if it had not been for the two-twenty-three I should have liked to ask him a few questions. I should have asked him, for example, how he would assure the safety of his one beloved spot of earth, that little circle of hills, without assuring that of Litchfield County, and how Litchfield County could get along without Connecticut, or Hartford without Washington. Doubtless he would have had some persuasive if not adequate answers, for I myself can think of several; but my time for talking any topic to a conclusion, or for thinking any problem even half-way through, was over.

The major said that the casualties of the Great War had been grossly underestimated, that in order to reach the right figure we must add to the millions killed or maimed in body all the millions more who came back hopelessly crippled in mind and soul. He thought the most pitiful of all these 'casualties' were the men who never saw an hour of action, never learned by ocular and olfactory observation — the only thing that can teach such people — what war is. These young men, he said, had been sent back into civil life by the hundred thousand with all the poison systematically pumped into them by the propagandists still working. It would work in them through all their lives, and to the third and fourth generations. They would never find out that they had been fed upon lies. Knowing nothing when the war began, they learned nothing from it except the technic of coercion, suppression, prohibition, and propaganda. When a sensible man remembers all this, he said, he does not wonder at what has happened since the War in America. He foresaw it.

The major spoke with such enthusiasm that his pipe went out three or four times in ten minutes. He did nearly all the talking because I was munching raisins, and had, anyhow, few objections to make. While he was fumbling for another match I rose, twitched my knapsack into position, and took up my stick.

'Must you go?' he asked.

I told him that I had to catch a train at Norfolk in an hour and ten minutes.

'You might just do it,' he said rather dubiously, 'by running most of the way.'

I answered that I expected to do just that.

'But why,' the major asked, 'need you catch that train at all?'

It was precisely the sort of question I had asked of the good citizen with the rake — a very disconcerting question because it cut down to fundamentals and loosened a stone or two in our elaborate structure of make-believe. It was the kind of question never asked among serious-minded men. Briefly, it was an *uncivilized* question. I refused to answer it — not, of course, because I couldn't, but because there wasn't time. For the major was not the man to be put off with vague references to committee meetings and the like. He was quite capable of asking, 'Why committees?' — and then, or soon after, I should have been obliged to do some thinking. I belonged to the great army of men who waste no time in thinking and have no patience with first principles but who 'act, act in the living present' — or rather, I was rejoining my regiment. I suddenly felt a wave of exasperation at this dreamy idler lying under a tree in the middle of the day with a book of poems in his pocket and a cooling pipe in his mouth. His kind of talk might be all right, perhaps, for those who could afford it, but I had serious work to do in the real world. Bidding him a slightly abrupt farewell, I waded back to the lane through the rusty goldenrod. It was fifteen minutes past one o'clock. I began to run.

Running with a knapsack that flaps and jangles and jolts at every step is not my idea of a good time, particularly if the road is full of ruts. I did not find it interesting to do, and cannot make it seem interesting in the account. After a mile of it I came to Wangum Lake, a beautiful sheet of water nearly fourteen hundred feet above sea level and surrounded by woods. This is Norfolk's reservoir, and the good people of that town command you on nearly every other tree not to pollute its waters, suggesting various improbable ways in which you might do so but threatening unpleasant consequences if you adopt any one of them.

One of the guardians of this water was jolting down

a cross-road in a Ford just as I came to the lake. Seeing that I had less than an hour in which to cover five miles of uneven ground, I asked him in an insinuating way whether he was going to Norfolk. He slowed down, looked me deliberately over from my hatless head to my dusty shoes, taking special note of my walking-stick, and then, with an affirmative nod, put on speed and went round the bend in a cloud of dust. This was the cut direct. It left me wondering, half angry and half amused, for a long time. I felt that I had been paid in full for all I had ever said against automobiles and the people who run them. He had room for three passengers and must have seen that I was way-worn and carried a heavy pack. He might even have guessed that I had some reason for wanting to reach Norfolk as soon as possible. But there was something in my appearance that he did not like. I prefer to think that it was the walking-stick.

So I got no help whatever on my last five miles. They cost me more effort than all the rest of my two weeks' journey together. I ran very nearly the whole way, toward the end of it on hard pavement, with the contents of my knapsack — which included a very sharp-edged camera — jingling, flapping, thumping and thudding against my back. For a mile or so I carried the unwieldy bundle under one arm so as to avoid the monotonous thump and din, but, finding this more awkward still, I thrust my arms into the straps again and lumbered on. I was a grotesque spectacle, and I knew it. One who walks much in the country in these days soon grows accustomed to being stared at; he learns to take what I may call 'the automobile face' for granted, even though he may continue to feel that the mixture of amusement and superiority on many of the faces that hurtle by him is one of the less amiable expressions of the human countenance. I had long been inured to this; but to be really ridiculous, not only in the eyes of others but in my own, was another thing. The dogs went wild when I appeared on the out-

skirts of Norfolk. People hurried to the windows to watch me go by as they did to watch John Gilpin. I could see the curtains fly up here and there and the faces of women and children peer forth. Men digging in the fields or raking leaves in their gardens paused suddenly with their tools suspended in air to watch my transit, and one or two of them shouted after me words that I did not hear. Probably they all think I am insane, I thought, seeing me stagger through the dignified streets of Norfolk in this wild way — hatless, breathless, red in the face, ready to drop, with a knapsack raising welts across my back and an ash stick waving in the wind — but they don't know that I'm running to catch the Two-Twenty-Three, that I *must* catch the Two-Twenty-Three,

That I
Must catch
The Two-Twenty-Three,
The Two . . .
Twenty . . .
Three . . .
The Two-
Twen-
Tythree.

This nauseous jingle somehow lodged and stuck in my head, reverberating to a tune I particularly abhor, in spite of my violent efforts to dislodge it. Through all the hours of torment that I crowded into the next ten minutes the words and the tune clung to me. My brain had to have something to distract its attention from the pain in my legs and feet, the sharper pain in my lungs, and the frightening speed of my heart. I tried hard to switch over into 'Jog on, jog on, the footpath way,' but it was no go. That merry song had served me well at other times, but it was not for these uses, and so back I came to

I
Must
Catch
The Two
Twenty
Three!

It was disgusting, it was shameful that a man's brain should play him a trick like this, I thought — and a brain, too, that had been so chatty and pleasant until just now that something cheerful was needed more than ever. It ought to know that heart and lungs and legs were doing their uttermost. Once, to be sure, it tossed me a fleeting image of Pheidippides dropping dead after his run from Marathon, but this was hardly helpful, and immediately after it the song returned. And then, just as my second wind was dying in agony and I was battling for the third, the road, which had been down hill nearly all the way from the schoolhouse, began to climb. I was forced back into a trot, and watched the minutes whirl on my wrist-watch. Eight minutes . . . seven . . . six . . . and then a cross-roads. The wrong turning here would mean the loss of all my

effort, and I did not know which way to take. Two hundred yards ahead was a woman with a child, walking slowly away from me. I ran those two hundred yards, uphill, and stammered out a breathless question which she fortunately understood. She pointed straight on. . . . 'How far?' . . . 'Half a mile.' . . . Five minutes. . . . And then I fell into a dream about somebody running, somebody who had been running for months and years and who had forgotten how to stop. He was running up hill now, so that the knapsack he

carried did not jolt quite so painfully against his spine,
but I could see that he had hardly an atom of energy
left and I expected at every moment that he would drop
before my eyes. Yet on he went. On and up. It was
splendid. It was pathetic. It was insane. He reached
the village green, staggered up the steep hill past the
church, and then crossed the road toward the center, missing an automobile by inches. . . . The shrill
whistle of the in-coming train aroused me, and I knew
again that it was I who was running, I who felt the
pain. No matter. I could manage. I had felt that pain
before — in boyhood, playing at hare-and-hounds —
cycling over the hills of Devonshire — oh, many times.
Now for it. All depended on the next few seconds.
Rounding the corner, I saw that the train had come to
a stand. How long had it been standing? How long
would it wait? I put forth the last bit of strength I
could find. The world went blue before me. My heart
pumped like the shuttle of a sewing machine. And
then, when I was still one hundred feet away, the engine ohot up a huge column of steam, the wheels re-
volved, the train began to move. I tried to shout, but
could not make a sound. For half a second I gave it up,
acknowledged defeat, and slowed to a walk. I had done
what I could do. But then came a vision of the road
from Salisbury, and another vision, all in a flash, of the
longer road from Brooklyn far off in Windham County,
with this train at the end of it all. I would not have defeat to remember as the end of such a fortnight of
victorious living as this had been. Out of the reservoir

of energy we all have beneath the last atom of our strength came the strength I needed. I remember reaching out for the iron rail of the rear platform of the last car, swinging up the steps as in a dream, stumbling and fumbling in the pitch darkness of the coach for a seat, and then . . . oblivion for half an hour.

But I had returned to the twentieth century. I had caught the two-twenty-three.

THE END